INDONESIAN ART

TREASURES OF
THE NATIONAL MUSEUM, JAKARTA

INDONESIAN ART

TREASURES OF
THE NATIONAL MUSEUM, JAKARTA

Photography by
TARA SOSROWARDOYO

PERIPLUS
EDITIONS

Published in 1998 by
Periplus Editions (HK) Ltd
Editorial office:
5 Little Road #08-01
Singapore 536983

*The publication of this book was made possible through the generous support
of the following sponsors:*

P.T. Makindo
P.T. Bahana
Bakrie Group
P.T. Satelindo
Mr Jack Wijaya
P.T. Jardine Fleming
Mr Amir Abdul Rachman
P.T. Multimedia Nusantara

Editorial Co-ordinator: Suwati Kartiwa, *Director of
  the National Museum*
Production Co-ordinator: Mr Tjetjep Suparman
Motivator: Mr Joop Avé
General Editor: Edi Sedyawati
Project Administrator: Seti-Arti Kailola
Administrative support, Jakarta: Arief and Dian

Photographer: Tara Sosrowardoyo
Editors: Diana Darling, Jill A. Laidlaw
Translator: Linda Owens
Designer: Tan Seok Lui
Picture Editor: Peter Schoppert

Photographs © 1998 Tara Sosrowardoyo
Text and layout © 1998 Editions Didier Millet Pte Ltd

Designed and produced by
Editions Didier Millet Pte Ltd
593 Havelock Road, #02-01/02,
Singapore 169641
for **Buku Antar Bangsar**
Jarkarta

Distributors

Indonesia
PT Wira Mandala Pustaka
(Java Books - Indonesia)
Jalan Kelapa Gading Kirana
Blok A14 No. 17
Jakarta 14240

Southeast Asia
Berkeley Books Pte. Ltd
5 Little Road #08-01,
Singapore 536983

United States, United Kingdom, Europe
Charles E. Tuttle Co. Inc.
RRI Box 231-5, North Clarendon
VT 05759-9700

ISBN: 962-593-320-4

Printed and bound in Singapore by Star Standard Industries (Pte) Ltd

Photographs on preceding pages:
Half title, a shadow puppet (Wayang Kulit) from Cirebon, West Java;
frontispiece: Ardhanari, a portrait statue from Surabaya.

Photographs on following pages:
Page 6, detail of a Late Classic Era relief depicting a four-armed goddess; page 7, Amoghapasa
surrounded by his attendants, a gift to a Sumatran kingdom or province from the Javanese king
Visvarupakumara (1286); page 8, Kalimantan Siva; page 9, carving from Candi Jago, Malang, East Java
(thirteenth/fourteenth century).

CONTENTS

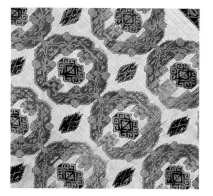

A NATIONAL MUSEUM FOR THE 21ST CENTURY

The National Museum has long served as an institution whose job is to collect, preserve, and present, in permanent and temporary exhibits, objects that constitute the cultural legacy of our nation. Due to the lack of any significant efforts at improvement or expansion, however, the current building of the National Museum has come to be increasingly inadequate. Growing demands on the National Museum mean that there must be a plan for managing its development in a comprehensive manner, and this plan must encompass both organisational and physical development. Synergy between these two elements is crucial as improvements of a piecemeal nature will not ensure the National Museum's ability to fulfil its role.

The existing structure of the National Museum, measuring approximately 11,500 square meters, is of great historical value—the main building dates to 1862. The development and construction of the new building began in mid-1996 and is due to be completed early in the year 2000. The area of the museum site, originally measuring 13,840 square metres, has been enlarged by 11,360 square metres to the north and south of the existing plot, to give a total of almost 25,000 square metres. On this land two new structures will be built: Buildings B and C. Building B, to be located on the north side of the existing building, will contain two basement levels and seven floors, encompassing 30,000 square metres. Building C, which will be located in a section of Building B, will have two basement levels and 10 floors, and measure 40,000 square metres.

This physical expansion will enable the

Museum to accommodate its activities fully. Approximately 40 per cent of the area will be allocated for permanent and temporary exhibit space and storage. Another 30 per cent will be for public use, including a lobby and auditorium; and for public services, such as a cafeteria, souvenir shop, and bookstore. The remaining 30 per cent will house offices and support areas, such as laboratories and rooms for conservation, preparation, photography, and collection study.

With these improvements, the job entrusted to the Museum—that of representing the nation's culture—will be performed more effectively. There will be attractive and interesting exhibits that can be easily understood by both Indonesian and foreign visitors. Attractive layout and interior design, the clear direction of visitors as they circulate through the exhibit areas, and a hierarchical arrangement of the interior space—these are just a few of the factors that will make for a more successful National Museum.

The National Museum is one of the main tourist destinations in Jakarta, the nation's capital. As the only centre for the exhibition of Indonesian cultural artefacts, it is a unique destination. Its strategic location on Jakarta's north-south historical axis makes it a landmark

Top: the Neo-Classical facade of the National Museum.

Below: the elephant statue originally given to the City of Batavia by King Chulanlongkorn of Thailand.

with great potential as a tourist destination. To meet the increase in both foreign and domestic tourist numbers, improvements in the physical quality of the National Museum to meet international standards are timely.

It goes without saying that physical expansion of the Museum is only part of the effort, and it must be accompanied by any necessary reorganization and the creation of activities that will motivate the general public to become devoted supporters of the Museum. Besides the scientific aspect appropriate to the National Museum's educative-cultural function, we must also consider its recreational aspect. Various recreational activities take place periodically: this part of the Museum's programme is carried out in conjunction with various organizations and community groups, and its aim is to attract visitors and increase community participation in the Museum's activities.

The Museum's collections reveal important information on the Indonesian people's cultural history—from the prehistoric period, through the classical period of the fourth to fifteenth centuries, to the rising influence of the Islamic religion in the sixteenth century, and the period of European influence beginning around the seventeenth century.

Cultures from the whole of Indonesia are represented: 525 different ethnic groups, inhabiting 17,000 islands large and small, from Sabang to Merauke. The diverse objects in the Museum's collections reveal the cultural values of the Indonesian people and the historical values of the nation. They reflect evidence of environmental wisdom from the prehistoric period, as well as sophisticated traditional technologies from the classical period, as seen in the temple structures at Borobudur, Prambanan, and Kalasan. Sculptures from the times of Hindu and Buddhist influence often reflect religious values in addition to aesthetic concerns.

An ethnic group's cultural values—the Indonesian people's regard for mutual aid and assistance is an example—are reflected in its daily life, in rituals connected with the harvest, and in the building of ceremonial structures,

places of worship, and community meeting places. Its ethical values are reflected in its communal and clan relationships. And its aesthetic values, which are inseparable from functional values, are contained in all of its works.

The 109,363 items collected by the National Museum from the 18th century up to the present day reflect these noble ideals and the richness of the Indonesian people's cultures. The collection is divided into several disciplines, including Prehistory, Archeology, History, Geography, Anthropology, Visual Arts, and Education.

The Museum should be able to satisfy the public's needs on both a national and a global scale. As part of its endeavour to advance into the arena of international museum activity, the National Museum must improve its facilities so that it becomes on a par with museums outside Indonesia. The developments now taking place anticipate future growth in regional and international relationships between museums.

As we approach the 21st century, it is hoped that the National Museum can improve both its image and its performance of the role with which it has been entrusted. The construction of new museum buildings should go a long way to achieving these twin aims.

New developments at the National Museum represented in the form of an architectural model.

Museum
Batavia

THE HISTORY OF THE NATIONAL MUSEUM

T he National Museum, as we currently understand it, comprises the building and its various collections, located on Jalan Merdeka Barat in Jakarta. The National Museum did not always belong to the Government of Indonesia. On the contrary, what is now the National Museum belonged for most of its history, to a private organisation, called the *Bataviaasch Genootschap van Kunsten en Wetenschappen* or the Batavian Society of Arts and Sciences. This Society was established on April 24, 1778, during the Dutch colonial period, and continued to exist until the early sixties, albeit under a different name. The National Museum building, with its white Neo-classical façade and Doric columns, used to be called *Gedung Gadjah*, after the statue of the elephant located in the forecourt, given to the City of Batavia in 1871 by King Chulalongkorn of Thailand.

From the end of the war for Indonesia's Independence (about 1949), until the final departure of the Dutch (1963), the Society continued to operate as a private organisation. It was governed by a board consisting of respected academics (in the beginning board members were Dutch and Indonesian and towards the end they were entirely Indonesian), intent on preserving a historical legacy built up over a period of almost 200 years. During a meeting of all members, on January 26, 1950, it was decided to change the name of the Society to *Lembaga Kebudajaan Indonesia, Koninklijk Bataviaasch Genootschap van Kunsten en Wetenschappen*, and in 1958 this was shortened to simply *Lembaga Kebudajaan Indonesia*. In 1963, due to increasing difficulties in managing its affairs, the Government was asked by the Society to take over the responsibility for the museum, and its collections and major libraries. Moh. Amir Sutaarga, then Secretary of the Society's Board of Directors, was instrumental in transferring all the Society's assets to the Ministry of Education and Culture. The transfer was further facilitated by the fact that the President of the Board, Prof. Dr. R. Prijono, was also the Minister for Education and Culture. The Society's museum, and its collections, have become the Indonesian National Museum, while the Society's collection of books and rare manuscripts became part of Indonesia's National Library.

In view of the very close relationship between the Society and its museum, understanding the history of the National Museum is really synonymous with understanding the history of the Society. Furthermore, to gain insight into questions such as the origin and nature of today's collections, it is necessary to consider the evolution of the Society over time. One must develop an understanding of the objectives and attitudes of the members of the Society, as well as the cultural context of Indonesia throughout the Society's existence.

Previous pages: An early photograph of the Society's collection of classical era statues from throughout Indonesia: in the foreground Ganesha, God of Wisdom and Learning, Son of Shiva and Parvati, from Candi Banon (Central Java).

Above: The Javanese laid unsuccessful siege to Batavia in 1629.

GENESIS

Various factors came together in the establishment of the Batavian Society of Arts and Sciences. Perhaps the most important element was the influence of the intellectual revolution known as the Enlightenment. This 18th-century movement originated in Europe, particularly in England, Italy and Germany, but most of all in France. It was marked by a questioning of tradition and a growing trend towards individualism, empiricism, and attempts at scientific reasoning.

The Enlightenment built upon foundation stones laid a century before by thinkers such as René Descartes (1596-1650), John Locke (1632-1704), Isaac Newton (1643-1727), Gottfried Wilhelm Leibniz (1646-1716) and Baruch Spinoza (1632-77). However, it was during the 18th century that new ideas and attitudes began to pervade many areas of thought, ultimately leading to the French Revolution in 1789. For example, between 1751 and 1772, Diderot and d'Alembert published their *Encyclopédie*, which, among other publications, criticised existing institutions, and exalted the arts and crafts and a liberal bourgeois society. In many other areas, scientific reasoning came to the forefront. In economic thought, the basis of modern economics was established when Adam Smith published in 1776 his famous work, *An Inquiry into the Nature and Causes of the Wealth of Nations*, with its advocacy of free trade and *laissez-faire* policies. The latter ethos stood in sharp contrast to the mercantilistic approach towards trade practised by the Dutch in their colonies.

The changes in thought outlined above had a major influence in Holland, whose *Verenigde Oostindische Compagnie* or VOC, the United East Indies Company, controlled the East Indies archipelago, the modern-day Republic of Indonesia. In 1752 a society of sciences, the *Hollandsche Maatschappij der Wetenschappen*, was established in Haarlem, the Netherlands. The first major factor leading to the establishment of a society in Batavia came in the form of a competition organised in 1771 by the *Hollandsche Maatschappij der Wetenschappen*, calling for essays focused on Dutch trade, with particular emphasis on the East Indies, and on how the arts and sciences could play a role in promoting Christianity in the colonies.

The second important factor which led to the establishment of a society can be found in the person of Jacob Cornelis Mattheus Radermacher, who by all accounts can be considered the founder of the Batavian Society. Radermacher, son of a prominent Dutch family, started working for the VOC in 1757, at the age of 16. In the years that followed he rose rapidly through the company's hierarchy. His marriage to the stepdaughter of a high company official, Reinier de Klerk, Director-General of the VOC, clearly helped. (De Klerk was the first occupant of a beautiful mansion in Batavia, today the National Archives on Jalan Gajah Mada.)

RADERMACHER
Radermacher's beliefs and attitudes, perhaps strongly influenced by developments in Europe of which he undoubtedly had read, were quite different from those of the majority of VOC officials. The second half of the 18th century saw the rapid decline of the once-powerful VOC in Asia. Governor-Generals in Batavia after 1760 were older men who had risen slowly within the narrow hierarchy of company officials. Faced with the company's declining fortunes, they tended to make profit their sole goal, while covering their own shortsightedness and bigotry with elaborate rituals emphasising rank and status. Intellectual activity was rare among company officials and the subdued group of 'burghers' and military. Censorship of books and the absence of printed news contributed to a prevailing atmosphere of disinterest among the majority of people. Corruption among VOC officials was extensive in those times, as was documented by an ex-VOC secretary, P. van Dam. However, at the time these findings were kept secret, contributing to a general atmosphere of secrecy and distrust.

In spite of these conditions, Radermacher and a very small group of like-minded individuals believed in a better future. Characteristic was his membership of the Freemasons, an international society adhering to principles of brotherliness, charity and mutual aid. Freemasonry seemed to offer Radermacher an opportunity for some kind of

A View of Batavia, the Capital of the Dutch Settlements in India – an early view of Batavia from the sea.

The Batavia residence of the Dutch Governor-General in an engraving of 1882. This illustration is from volume two of a book depicting life in the Dutch East Indies by Van Rees.

social and intellectual activity in Batavia's bleak society. Radermacher was the key founder of the first Masonic lodge in Batavia in 1762. The building used to house the lodge still exists on Jalan Budi Utomo in Central Jakarta. In 1763 Radermacher departed for the Netherlands, where he remained for over three years. During this period he gained a doctorate in law and became exposed to, and involved in, the intellectual debates raging within the Netherlands. He undoubtedly learned about the *Hollandsche Maatschappij der Wetenschappen*, with its enlightened views.

Upon his return to Batavia in 1767, Radermacher's initial intention was to found a society similar to the *Hollandsche Maatschappij der Wetenschappen*. However, his proposal was considered 'unheard of' and 'impossible to achieve' by Batavian society, which for all practical purposes consisted only of VOC officials. Consequently, the idea was shelved until some ten years later. At that time, on the occasion of its 25th anniversary on May 21, 1777, the *Hollandsche Maatschappij der Wetenschappen* in Haarlem decided to establish a branch dealing with economic questions, which would also operate in the Dutch overseas territories. The Governor-General, the Director-General (not Reinier de Klerk at that time) and Radermacher were appointed Directors in the Indies. It is not particularly clear what actually transpired regarding this decision but the issue of the establishment of a learned society in Batavia resurfaced due to the attention drawn

by the *Hollandsche Maatschappij der Wetenschappen* ruling.

Radermacher's father-in-law became Governor-General of the VOC in October 1777 and Radermacher and a few others were now ready to proceed with the establishment of a society. However, an independent society was preferred over a branch of the *Hollandsche Maatschappij der Wetenschappen*. The great distance from Europe as well as the specific issues faced in the East Indies made the founding of the economic branch unfeasible, according to Radermacher. Instead, they preferred a separate society to investigate properly the economy of the Dutch Indies. This could also generate interest on the part of the Haarlem Society in focussing on the whole of the Dutch Indies, and not just on issues of an economic nature.

The founding of the Batavian Society of Arts and Sciences officially took place on April 24, 1778. De Klerk, then Governor-General of the VOC, and all the other high officials present in Batavia signed up as directors, while a large number of the most prominent citizens became members. The Society chose as its motto: *Ten Nutte van het Algemeen*, indicating that it would work for 'The Public Benefit'. It is interesting to note that the Society in Batavia was the first of its kind in all of Asia. In India, where the British East India Company was the equivalent of the VOC, the Asiatic Society of Bengal was established in Calcutta in 1784, six years after the Batavian Society.

THE HISTORY OF THE SOCIETY

Throughout its almost 200-year history, the overriding goal of the Society was to analyse, through scientific research and scholarship, every cultural aspect of the East Indies colony and its people. The results of the Society's work are encapsulated in the 79 volumes of the Society's *Transactions*, published between 1779 and 1950. They contain more than 31,000 pages of text, covering a very broad array of subjects, ranging from such practical areas as new irrigation methods, to the most detailed analyses of old Javanese texts. The *Transactions* constitute a veritable treasure trove with respect to the archipelago's rich cultural history.

In addition, from 1853 through to 1952, the Society published the *Tijdschrift voor Indische taal- land- en volkenkunde*, or the *Journal of Languages and Ethnography of the Indies*, while from 1926 through to 1951 the Society published a *Jaarboek*, a compilation of mostly scholarly material, published on an annual basis. Critical to the scholarship conducted by the Society was its collection of artefacts, old manuscripts, archeological finds and other items found throughout the archipelago. The collection housed in the National Museum is the result of numerous initiatives taken by individual members of the Society.

Throughout its history the Batavian Society of Arts and Sciences had its ups and downs. The fluctuating state of the Society was not just a result of external circumstances, but also due to the fact that its member-scholars only remained for a limited time in the colony. Whenever a scholar with a particular interest left the Indies for home, it frequently created a hiatus, until someone else took up an interest in the same subject. Despite these interruptions it can be said that the Society became the focal point for serious cultural research on the archipelago; the Society was the place where new scientific initiatives were taken, and a place which functioned as an 'advisory board' over cultural issues. This was especially important in the early days when there were no government bureaus dealing with, for example, archeological issues, let alone universities. The Dutch Government only belatedly recognised the importance of the Society, when it bestowed the appellation *Koninklijk*, or Royal, on the Society in 1923.

MAIN PERIODS

In very broad terms one can identify three main periods in the Society's history. During these times significant momentum was built, which kept the Society functioning until its demise in 1962. It is interesting to note that each of these periods is associated with one particular person, who had the vision and energy to mobilise others for 'The Public

Benefit'. First, there was the period of the Society's founding during which Radermacher and his colleagues gave form to the Society's work. This period was relatively short, from 1778 until about 1794, when 'scientific production' came to a halt with Radermacher's untimely death. He was killed in a mutiny aboard ship when he returned to Holland in 1782, and this undoubtedly robbed the Society of much vitality.

The second period coincided with the British Interregnum during 1811-1816, when the troops of the British East India Company drove the Dutch out of the East Indies, and Sir Thomas Stamford Raffles not only became Lieutenant-Governor of Java, but also accepted the Presidency of the Society (in 1813).

The third period started during the 1830s and lasted until 1940. During this period the Batavian Society became a world-renowned scientific organisation, famous for its work in ethnography, anthropology and the languages of the Indonesian Archipelago. More than any one else, Dr. W. R. Baron van Hoëvell was the intellectual force behind the Society's renewal in the middle of the last century, leading up to the most productive period for the Society, which was during the first four decades of this century.

During each of the above-mentioned periods the specific activities of the Society's members and the scope of their work varied a great deal. However, it was during the first relatively short period that the inquisitive nature and scientific orientation of the Society was firmly established. Although the founders had to tread very carefully in order not to interfere overtly with the very secretive VOC, a charter was set up calling for an increase in the amount of knowledge about the colony. It was stated that the Society would stimulate all arts and sciences and would eagerly receive anything which dealt with the natural history, antiquities, customs and mores of the people in the colony. Hence, the first volumes of the *Transactions* dealt with such broad subjects as natural sciences, ethnography, history, literature, medicine, and agriculture. In addition, in true keeping with the spirit of the age, the charter

Europe recreated in the capital of the Netherlands' possessions in the East Indies. Neoclassical architecture and French garden design were faithfully transplanted to the tropical heat of Batavia.

stipulated that the Society would make the subjects of its investigations benefit agriculture, trade, and the welfare of the settlements. This very practical and pragmatic approach to the application of the arts and sciences was further highlighted by the practice of soliciting answers to specific questions in various areas. The resulting answers would be rewarded with a cash prize. In volume I of the *Transactions* (1779), 46 questions were listed: 23 dealing with agriculture, 2 with fishing, 8 with industry, 8 with mechanics, 3 with medicine, and 2 with literature. As it turned out this method of soliciting interest in the Society met with a limited response. Primarily the Society's members wrote essays for the *Transactions*, with Radermacher, as the presiding officer of a member-committee overseeing the day-to-day work, one of the key contributors.

This very broad, and what could be called liberal, approach towards the Society's work was also reflected in its initial membership. When the Society began its work there was a core of 103 members in Batavia, of which one-third were members of the Freemason movement. In addition, there were 77 members from outside the VOC's East Indies 'capital', including the company's possessions and stations in India, Ceylon (modern-day Sri Lanka), the Cape of Good Hope in Southern Africa, and Japan. Finally, there were a small number of corresponding members, residing mostly in the Netherlands.

It is interesting to note that although the Society was set up as a private organisation, outside the VOC, it was not far removed from the VOC's influence. In fact, in the beginning the Chief Director of the Society had to be the Governor-General, a VOC position, while only high government officials could serve as Directors.

On 24 April, 1778, Radermacher and 11 other VOC officials signed a document establishing the Batavian Society for Arts and Sciences, the first of its kind in Asia.

DEVELOPMENTS IN EUROPE

Decline of the Society's fortunes after the death of Radermacher coincided with violent events in Europe, specifically the Napoleonic Wars. Napoleon Bonaparte (1769-1821) invaded and occupied the Netherlands, driving out Prince William V. The Dutch East Indies became French property, and on December 31, 1799 it was decreed that the VOC be disbanded. Although there were sporadic meetings during these years, it can be said that scientific zeal seemed to have left the Society. The only bright light was provided by Dr. Thomas Horsfield, an American botanist, who visited Java from 1799 to 1800, and returned in 1801 for an extended stay. The Society elected him as a member and facilitated his research on Java. However, they could not offer much more in the way of assistance, and none of Horsfield's contributions appeared in print, because of a lack of printing facilities at the time.

While France occupied Holland, and thus the Dutch East Indies, the British East India Company, headquartered in India, became very concerned about the French-Dutch colonialists in the East Indies, who by now were Britain's enemies. Sir Thomas Stamford Raffles, the company's representative in Penang, was in constant communication with Lord Minto, the Governor-General and highest-ranking company official outside London. Their concern was that no enemy should disturb trade through the Indian Ocean and the South China Sea to China. They both saw the monopolistic practices of the French-Dutch enemies in the East Indies as a serious threat to British trade. And so the plan was made to invade Java. According to Raffles it would be best if all the company's possessions in the Indies could be incorporated in a new unitary structure, centred in Batavia or noted: 'With the year 1838 the Dutch Indies entered a new era.' The colony saw the arrival of a large number of well-educated Government officials and scholars from Holland. Equally importantly, this new era was characterised by the emergence of numerous journals and magazines of significant intellectual content, as well as the establishment of various professional organisations. Undoubtedly made possible by a more favourable economic climate, these developments were testimony that the nature of society in the Dutch Indies was rapidly changing for the better. It was at that time, for example, that *Het Natuur- en Geneeskunding Archief voor Nederlandsch-Indië*, the *Science and Medical Archives for the Dutch Indies*, was published for the first time. Simultaneously, around this time professional organisations in the area of physics as well as medicine were established. This period also saw, for example, the emergence of the Dutch Indies Teachers Association.

NEW DIRECTIONS

The important consequence of the above developments was that, where in the past the Batavian Society had been the only organisation of its kind, covering all scientific endeavours, there was now a variety of intellectual and scientific efforts going on in the Dutch Indies. On the one hand, this resulted in increased activity by the Society, because the climate for its own work had significantly improved. On the other hand, the Society was now in a position to focus more clearly on what it could do best, given that there were other organisations, specialising in specific areas, who could shoulder the load of pursuing the application of arts and sciences for 'The Public Benefit'. Thus the Society, slowly but surely, could take up a position as the one central, overarching scientific organisation in the colony, supported by other, smaller, more specialised organisations. This provided the Society with the opportunity to improve greatly the quality of its scholarship and publications, although access of the general public to the Society's work was necessarily reduced. It also allowed the Society to improve greatly its standing in the international scientific community, to the point where it became one of the most outstanding scientific organisations in culture-related sciences in the world.

The new direction for the Society was most vigorously pursued by Dr. W.R. Baron van Hoëvell. His influence lasted almost ten years, first as a member of the Board of Directors from 1839 to 1842, and subsequently as Vice President and later as President until 1848. By profession a minister in the church and not a Government official, he was an outstanding scholar and politician. Academically orientated and possessing drive, skill, and intellectual curiosity about Java's cultural past, he had the ability to note achievements and gaps, and to set priorities accordingly. Under the favourable conditions described above it was the latter quality that was of immense value for the future of the Society.

In a major address, on October 5, 1843, van Hoëvell outlined the Society's main interests: language and literature, archeology and antiquities, ethnography and anthropology, and the natural sciences. However, he proposed that the natural sciences were to be de-emphasised, and that the focus of the Society should be exclusively on the first three areas. Furthermore, he proposed that the languages of the archipelago should be made the special subject of the Society's investigations, noting in particular the (then) recent interest of scholars in Europe. In doing so, he was very much aware of the importance of printing original Javanese and Malay manuscripts for the people of Java, and that efforts should be undertaken to stimulate their desire to read by making such texts readily available. Another field of activity that received major emphasis in van Ho'vell's 1843 address was the preservation of antiquities. He announced that to support governmental efforts an archeological collection (*Kabinet van Oudheden*) had been founded, in which each item would be carefully described and depicted.

In response to the direction set by van Hoëvell, a long period of serious scholarship followed in the areas he identified. For

A stone figure of Vishnu standing amongst the roots of a tree. This photograph is one in a series that Isodore Van Kinsbergen completed for the Society in the 1860s.

The National Museum around 1878, shortly after being built but 100 years after the Society's establishment, in the park-like setting of the *Koningsplein*, now Merdeka Square.

example, with respect to the study of languages, the Directors of the Society approached several Dutch specialists (in 1844), located in Yogyakarta and Surakarta, requesting assistance in selecting and translating important works from old Javanese. This initiative was highly successful. It encouraged a large number of subsequent studies conducted over a period of more than 50 years, as can be seen from the many manuscripts contained in the *Transactions* between 1844 and 1905. It is here, for example, that we find many annotated translations and studies. It is during this time that extremely important historical sources, such as the *Pararaton* and the *Nagarakertagama*, were discovered. The latter, obtained in a military raid on the Kraton of Lombok in 1894, was first transferred to the museum in Leiden, in the Netherlands. It was returned to Indonesia when Queen Juliana presented the manuscript to President Soeharto during her state visit in 1974, together with the famous statue of Prajnaparamita. This total body of works forms by itself an outstanding and unparalleled collection, describing Indonesia's cultural heritage.

Together with the study of languages, the study of antiquities was put on a solid footing. Efforts were made to list and reproduce lithographically all inscriptions found on Java, including a lithographic reproduction of the Borobudur monument, with all its statues and galleries. The explanatory texts were provided by the Society. Generally, these efforts were undertaken in close cooperation with the Government, with the Society providing the expertise to guarantee scientifically sound results. In fact, from the 1830s onwards the Government began to depend on the Society for the preservation of antiquities found throughout Indonesia. Under the administration of Governor-General J. C. Baud (1833-1836), officials in the various parts of the archipelago were instructed to assist in the creation of the Society's museum by looking for objects and transferring them to the museum. Subsequent decrees expanded these instructions. Most important was the 1855 Law of Treasure Trove, which stipulated that any archeological find was to be reported to the Government, which then usually provided the Society with an option to buy it at its appraised value. In 1931 this was further clarified in what was called the *Monumenten Ordinantie*, or regulations concerning the preservation of monuments.

REORGANISATION

Unlike the early days of the Society, the third important period, from 1830 until 1940, was virtually uninterrupted, with the Society fulfilling a most important role in preserving the cultural heritage of Indonesia. As time went by, the scientific work became more and more extensive, opening more and more areas of investigation. In addition, the time had long since passed when one Board of Directors could adequately deal with all the issues confronting the Society. During the latter part of the last century and the early part of this century, extensive discussions took place on how to cope with this increasing work load. These discussions revived a long-standing issue: whether the Society should be narrowly or broadly defined. Finally, in 1925 the Society was reorganised, and the decision was made to maintain a broad approach but to create different specialized, but independent, groups within the Society, each with its own Director. This led to the creation of a group for languages and ethnography, and one for *adat* law in 1926. In 1928 a group for law was established, as well as for political economy. In 1932, a group for

the study of international affairs was formed, while in 1938 a group for history emerged. World War II brought all of the Society's work to a complete halt. Most of the above groups were not reactivated after the war, and only the language and ethnography group and the history group were revived.

From the above summary of the Society's history one may conclude that, in particular during the latter part of its existence, the Society was a sizable and important organisation. And yet, membership of the Society has always been relatively modest, underscoring the point that most of the work was done by people who had a great personal interest, and were driven by intellectual curiosity. No large bureaucracy was instituted. Rather, most members were working members. They were scholars who themselves became intimately involved in the day-to-day business of the Society, driven by the desire to preserve the cultural heritage of what is now the Indonesian nation.

As earlier mentioned, at the time of the founding there were a total of 180 members. This rapidly declined after Radermacher's death. By 1814—the time of Raffles—the Society struggled back to a total membership of 72. Substantial recovery took place after that. By 1828 there were 99 members in the colony and 38 elsewhere. By 1853 these numbers had increased to 135 and 35 respectively. Around 1900 the number of members stood between 275 and 300, including those in and outside the colony. In 1940 there were a total of 324 members: 240 ordinary members, 19 special members, 9 corresponding members, 34

honorary members, 9 patron-type members and 13 members in the Board of Directors.

Finally, it is of interest to note that membership by native Indonesians goes back to 1860, when five Indonesians were members. One of these, the famous painter Raden Saleh, was elected an honorary member in 1866 after presenting the Society with a valuable collection of manuscripts and archeological objects. Among other things, he donated the now famous *Kebantenan* inscriptions (old inscribed bronze tablets from the Sundas) to the Society, and funded excavation on pre-historical sites in Central Java. Although Indonesian membership remained minimal, and initially was limited to members of the Javanese court circles, it gradually increased until it reached about 10% of the total membership by 1930. One particular Indonesian should be mentioned here: Prof. Dr. Hoesein Djajadiningrat. This outstanding scholar—linguist, historian and Islamic expert par excellence—was elected to the Society and became a member of the Board of Directors in 1915. In 1936 he was elected President of the Society, which he remained until his death on November 12, 1960.

THE SOCIETY'S MUSEUM: A REFLECTION OF ITS WORK

The development and maintenance of a museum had always been an integral part of the Society's work, although its specific function changed dramatically as the Society developed. In the early days the Museum was primarily a collection of 'curiosities', but it eventually evolved into a 'working laboratory' for the Society's main objective: the study and research of the cultural history of Indonesia, in all its aspects.

It was Radermacher who was instrumental in getting, not only the Society, but also the museum, off to a good start. He donated a house on Jalan Kali Besar which also contained eight cabinets filled with books, manuscripts, musical instruments, coins, dried plants and other curios. In effect, through this action he laid the foundation for the Society's art, botanical, numismatic and other collections. It

Above left: The Compagnie's Kamer or (East Indies) Company Room in the early 1900s, displaying the initial historical collection of the Museum, now part of Jakarta's Historical Museum.
Above: Indonesia's first world renowned painter, Raden Saleh (1807-1880), one of the earliest Javanese benefactors of the National Museum.

A museum employee looks on cautiously as a photographer documents the newly built museum.

should be noted that at the time the collection of art and curios was a favourite pastime for the upper classes, in both Asia and Europe. As a result, the VOC transported many items to Holland, such as porcelain, fine textiles and Chinese vases, while in the East Indies well-to-do people collected items from the West. For example, the Sultan of Makasar, Hassanudin, owned a collection of maps of Europe and the world, while other kings had other collections, such as clocks and watches made in Europe.

In fact, Radermacher's establishment of a curio cabinet was very much in line with similar efforts in Holland. Here, the Princes (*Stadhouders*) William IV and V, had established similar cabinets in their palace in the Hague, containing antiques from the colony, collections of dried plants used for botanical studies, preserved animals, etc. Early on, when Radermacher had asked Stadhouder William V to become the patron of the young Society, he had sent him a preserved orangutan from Borneo for his nature and art cabinet.

The Society's collection of rare items, established by Radermacher, steadily grew via donations of similar objects by other members. A special member of the Board was appointed with responsibility for finances, the library and the cabinets of 'natural items and other curios'. One of the Society's members even donated a small botanical garden, where the first conservator, the German Frederick Baron von Wurmb, experimented with different herbs, gave demonstrations with physics instruments and made meteorological observations.

In terms of the type of items collected by the Society's members, there was no real change over the first 50 or 60 years of its existence. However, as time went by the collection contained more and more items of lasting value. Still, the collections could certainly not be classified as a museum in the modern sense. What did change was the place where the cabinets were displayed. In 1814, during the second 'glory' period of the Society, under Raffles, all the cabinets were moved to a new home for the Society, located behind a special Government building, which was then called *Societeit de Harmonie*. The Society's new home was located on what is now Jalan Majapahit, in a building which has since been demolished to make room for the current buildings of the State Secretariat.

During the presidency of Commissary-General Du Bus de Gisighnies (1826-1830), a plan was made to construct a special building that could house the entire collection. However, lack of funds prevented the realisation of this plan. The same plans were revived under the administration of Governor-General J.-C. Baud (1833-1836), who was considerably more sympathetic towards the Society. He allowed some of the rooms of the *Harmonie* to be used for what was then the archeological and ethnological parts of the collection. He also provided the Society with an annual sum of 2,400 guilders for the upkeep of the museum. In addition, he was instrumental in making it possible for the Society to establish an extensive zoological collection of preserved animals from all over the archipelago, including mammals, birds, molluscs, and other animals.

STRENGTHENING THE COLLECTION

Despite the government's efforts to assist the Society, the overall status of the museum was less than satisfactory, with its collections spread over at least two locations. Therefore, in 1836, the Board of Directors made the important decision to establish a 'real' museum for natural history, history, and ethnography. Coinciding with this decision, however, was the growing awareness that the natural history collection, including the zoological collection, required more funds for its upkeep than the Society had available. Hence, efforts to maintain and expand this collection were more or less suspended, and finally in 1843 it was decided to disband the zoological collection; part went to the Rijksmuseum in Leiden and part was publicly auctioned off. This decision ended the Society's studies on the flora and fauna of the colony. A similar contraction of the collection took place in the mid-1850s when the mineralogical and geological parts of the collection were transferred to the newly established (1850) Society of Physics.

With these decisions, the natural history part of the collection was effectively eliminated, and the Society concentrated, from then on, on establishing a museum exclusively focused on its historical, ethnological and numismatic collections. In addition, of course, the Society maintained its library and its manuscript collection, with its extensive special collections of languages of the archipelago. Both the library and the manuscript collection have long contributed to the scientific importance of the Society. From around the turn of the century until World War II, the Society's library was among the largest, if not the largest, in Southeast Asia, taking on the character of a well-stocked university library for the social sciences.

Despite the Society's decision in 1836 to establish a new museum, it took 26 years before substantial progress was made. It was not until 1862 that King William III granted permission for the Director of Buildings of the colonial Government to build a permanent museum for the Society, which we now know as the National Museum. It is believed that construction of the building took perhaps three to four years. However, we know that on Sunday, September 22, 1867, the Board of Directors made their first visit to the newly constructed building, only to order still more changes. The record shows that on January 14, 1868, the Directors of the Society held their first official meeting in the new museum. At that time the building did not have a second floor, nor were there various rooms and spaces which we see today and which were added at later dates. It is interesting to note that the current building would not have been used as a museum if World War II had not intervened. In the 1930s there were plans to build a new museum in the vicinity of the current building, while the current building was destined to house only the Society's extensive library, together with the libraries of the then Faculty of Law and Faculty of Literature.

THE EXPANSION OF THE COLLECTION

When the Society occupied its new museum in 1868, the expansion of the collections accelerated. Through a variety of means the museum obtained more and more artefacts. Most came from private contributions, and some resulted from close cooperation between the colonial Government and the Society. In three instances artefacts included in the collection resulted from Dutch military raids. The contents of the Kratons of Lombok, Banten

Raden Saleh, one of the first Indonesian members of the Batavian Society, was admired for his mastery of painting in the European idiom. The size of Salen's house is testimony to his success and ample proof of his wealth.

Above: The Society's focus on studying Indonesia's cultural diversity is reflected in this photograph (from the early 1900s) showing the Museum's extensive ethnographic collection.

Opposite: An early view of the Museum.

and Banjarmasin were largely transferred to the museum, as a result of these raids. However, it is of interest, in this regard, that the other Kratons that still exist, such as in Solo and Yogyakarta, have maintained their own collection of valuable artefacts. In general, when Society members discovered items of great interest while travelling on business throughout Indonesia, they were able to convince Government officials that such items should be transferred to the Society's Museum. In particular the Government's archaeological office, established in 1913, was instrumental in expanding the collection. Over time, new departments of the museum were established, mostly as a result of the initiative of specific individuals.

At the beginning of this century Mr. and Mrs. Serrurier ten Cate were responsible for establishing the historical department, with a special section on European artefacts found in the Dutch Indies. In the 1930s this particular collection was considerably expanded by the then Secretary of the Society, and curator of several collections, van der Hoop. The ceramics collection was first established in 1932. This valuable collection consists of some 5,086 artefacts dating back as far as the Han Dynasty of the second century BC, up to and including the Ming Dynasty of the late 17th to 18th century. The majority of this collection was donated to the Museum by E. W. van Orsoy de

Flines, who was also its first curator until he left in 1957. He worked in Indonesia, first as a manager of a rubber plantation in Ungaran, near Semarang in Central Java, and later as a bank manager. One of the most important collections is that of the prehistoric department, which was originally established by its first curator Dr. P. V. van Stein Callenfels in 1933. It was the crowning achievement of many years of work. The collection consists of many special items, including stone implements, human fossils, golden masks, bronze kettledrums, ceremonial tools and implements, and many others.

By the beginning of World War II the collections in the museum had a decidedly ethnographic orientation, with particular emphasis on what has been called the classical period in Indonesia's history. This was very much a reflection of the interest of the Society's membership during the first 40 years of this century. There always had been much less interest in a more general historical perspective on Indonesia. The latter emerged more or less by accident when at the commemoration of the 300th anniversary of Batavia, in 1919, people started to explore the city's early history. A book, *Oud Batavia*, was published and a large exhibition was organised by the Society, with the assistance of archivist De Haan. This exhibition contained the beginning of a historical collection on Jakarta which was later transferred to a special branch of the museum, exclusively focused on Batavia. At the end of World War II the Society's main museum, at its present location, was known as Museum Pusat, while the branch museum evolved into what now is called the Museum Sejarah Jakarta on Taman Fatahillah in Central Jakarta. With the establishment of an independent Jakarta Historical Museum, under the direction of the City of Jakarta, the Museum Pusat subsequently became the National Museum.

THE NATIONAL MUSEUM

Overall, the National Museum contains an extensive and most valuable collection, built up over more than 200 years. It is the only Indonesian museum which is truly national. The total collection presently stands at some 110,000 individual pieces. The collection is extremely broad in scope, covering all of Indonesia's territory and virtually all of the country's history. It contains items from the prehistoric period of some 40,000 years ago, to the classical period between the 4th and 15th centuries, to the entry of Islam into Indonesia during the16th and 17th centuries, and reflects European historical influences from the 17th up to the 20th centuries. To classify its many items, the entire collection has been divided into nine major groups: Prehistoric; Archeological, including statues and relics from the Hindu and Buddhist periods; Numismatic and Heraldic, including one of the largest antique coin collections in the region; Historical, including many items dating from the VOC period; Geographical, including many old maps; Ethnographical, including many items of ethnic groups from Sumatra to Irian Jaya; Textiles, including many different types of textile from all over Indonesia; Ceramics; and Fine Arts, including many famous paintings from artists such as Raden Saleh and Abdullah.

In its totality the National Museum shows at its core the perspective of the scientists and scholars responsible for its early development. Some have said that the museum is one that mirrors the colonial era, and presents an 'ethnic map of greater Java when Indonesia was the Dutch Indies during the early twentieth century', reflecting a desire to learn about Indonesians. This stands in contrast to collections in some other museums in Indonesia with a more local character, such as the Sana Budaya Museum and Library in Yogyakarta. Within this perspective, the National Museum provides only a limited view of Indonesia's cultural history.

Others have emphasised the Eurocentric nature of the collections in the museum. Soedarmadji Damais in an essay in *Pusaka, Art of Indonesia*, entitled *Pusaka in Times of Change*, traces the history of *pusaka* or cultural objects with spiritual power. He relates this elusive quality to the type of objects which have been collected in Indonesia, and which constitute part of the content of the National Museum. The issue raised by Damais is that the

collection of cultural objects comprises objects of value from a Western perspective. He states:

'In traditional Indonesian societies, the importance of an object, natural or cultural, was not generally understood in terms of intrinsic or aesthetic value, nor even in terms of its antiquity. This is perhaps a more European idea. Traditionally, the Indonesian criterion of an object's value was the assumed degree of its *kesaktian* (spiritual power). A *keris* or a lance of no obvious beauty could be considered priceless if associated with a knight or ruler of kingdoms past. Stones or fragments of statues, regarded as endowed with *kesaktian*, were treated with great respect. This is the essence of the *pusaka* concept, originating far in the past and maintained to the present day.

'Sometimes, by coincidence, an Indonesian *pusaka* would be recognised by European connoisseurs as a masterpiece, but this is by no means always the case. Conversely, an object thought valuable by a Western collector on account of its beauty or antiquity may often be regarded with indifference by the traditional Indonesian mind. This indifference may help to explain why Indonesians, past and present, have little interest in archeological and historical remains which, in the West, would be regarded as part of the national heritage and treated accordingly. It will be seen, then, that the concept of *pusaka* and that of the "cultural object," the object whose status is based on its historic or artistic value, do not coincide.'

Subsequently, with respect to collections originally established by Europeans, or by Indonesians with a strong grounding in European art history, he states: 'Valuable as they are, these institutions, being museums in the conventional Western sense, are nonetheless products of an alien cultural sensibility. Impersonal collections of putative treasures, exposed to the public eye, shorn of ritual meaning, are a concept foreign to most Indonesians. Only a small minority, familiar with modern Western attitudes, can fully appreciate this form of presentation.'

Although the issues raised above are valuable in their own right, there is no doubt that the Museum of the Batavian Society of Arts and Sciences has given Indonesia a unique and valuable starting point for the continued development of a true National Museum. Among others, such a further development can already be seen in the expanding fine arts collection, begun after World War II. The challenge is to make full use of the opportunity that has already been given to the nation—to continue the development of a true National Museum for the people of Indonesia; a museum made by Indonesians for Indonesians. In this regard, the legacy of colonial days is merely the basis for Indonesians to learn about their own history. It is up to Indonesian art historians, ethnographers, archeologists, as well as representatives of other relevant disciplines, to continue the task of preserving Indonesia's culture for future generations, with the National Museum as the repository of their efforts.

Jakarta, September 12, 1997
H. E. Prof. Dr.-Ing. Wardiman Djojonegoro

Above: A stone figure of Vishnuin fine condition. From *Oudheten van Java*, photographed by Isodore van Kinsbergen.

Opposite: The frontispiece to C. L. Blume's botanical work, *Rumphia*, depicts a European sitting amongst Oriental antiquities of various kinds. This illustration is a good example of the European bias during the 19th century when conducting research into Asian antiquities and natural history.

This account was compiled from the following sources:
(a) Dr. P. Bleeker, *Overzigt der Geschiedenis van het Bataviaasch Genootshap van Kunsten and Wetenschappen van 1778-1853*;
(b) Lian The, Paul W. van der Veur, *The Verhandelingen van het Bataviaasch Genootschap: An Annotated Content Analysis*, 1973;
(c) A.J. Bernet Kempers, *Het Bataviaasch Genootschap van 1778*, 1978;
(d) Dr. Onghokham, *Asal-usul Museum Nasional*, Museum Jakarta Pusat, 1987.

The quotation from the essay 'Pusaka in Times of Change', by Soedarmadji Damais, is taken from *Pusaka, Art of Indonesia*, Editions Didier Millet, 1992, pp 205-208.

CHAPTER 1

ETHNOGRAPHY

T he instinct to venerate that which is powerful, and to adorn that which is revered, is common to human beings in all societies. It is the particular way in which they do so that distinguishes people and their cultures and that accounts for the great variety of man-made objects in all their uses, both sacred and for everyday use.

The National Museum's Ethnographic Collection comprises objects from ethnic groups throughout Indonesia, from Sabang Island at the western end of Sumatra to Merauke at the eastern border of Irian Jaya—over 300 ethnic groups, each with its own distinctive culture, including language, belief system, and art. This heterogeneity is the pride of the Indonesian nation, expressed in its national motto *Bhineka Tunggal Ika*, 'unity in diversity'.

The objects presented in this chapter were selected from among the Ethnographic Collection's 28,930 items, with particular regard for their artistic value.

The beauty of an art object lies not only in its aesthetic attributes—such as the appropriateness of form and material, the quality of its crafting, or the charm of its ornamentation—but also in the power of its symbolic meaning. While a work of art may be defined as something that expresses meaning through its pure existence and communicates the values of a society in a unique way, traditional art differs somewhat from the art of modern societies.

Spiritual might

In traditional societies, where every aspect of life is part of a collectively held system of meaning, there is no clear separation between the mundane and the spiritual. Art objects are nearly always associated with some ceremonial or practical activity. They are not deliberately devoid of function, as is the art of modern societies. Their symbology is communal—that is, it embodies a system of meaning that integrates individuals into their natural, social, and supernatural environment—whereas the art of modern societies tends rather to distinguish the individual in his environment.

Traditional works of art, in other words, often have a supernatural charge; and the fabrication, use, and care of these objects is felt to have a direct bearing on the welfare of the community. For example, when a Dayak artisan carves an *aso* motif (as seen in objects on pages 42-3), he invokes the power of a fearsome goddess; it is both an act of devotion and the creation of a new dwelling place for her. Certain textiles, and garments like the *epaku* on page 38, may be worn only by specific people for specific rituals. In Bali, where decoration and religion still coincide, the winged lion (on page 46) is as much a guardian figure as an architectural ornament.

Life music

Music, too, is a ritual art. Some of the traditional music of Indonesia is played on the gamelan—orchestras of various metallophone instruments that are frequently revered as repositories of spiritual power. The word 'gamelan' derives from the Javanese *gamel*—a type of hammer similar to those used by blacksmiths—and indicates the method of playing the instruments, by striking. Nearly all the instruments are percussive.

Gamelan music employs two different tuning systems: *slendro*, in which the octave is divided into five equal intervals; and *pelog*, a seven-tone scale with uneven intervals. The gamelan often accompanies dance, various forms of *wayang* performances, and rituals. Two gamelan orchestras are presented on pages 48-9.

The power of the dead

Because of the deep tradition of ancestor veneration throughout the archipelago, the magical aspect of art is perhaps most strongly felt in those objects associated with the dead. This is especially so of ancestral effigies, such as those from Leti (page 45) and the Dayak *hampatong* (page 36), which act as guardians and have wider attributes of divinity. The spirit effigy on page

38 formed part of a burial ritual that is no longer practised by the people from whom it originated. This rite, generally conducted a year after death, guided the soul from the temporary spiritual realm underground to the eternal heavenly realm, imagined as a high mountain. During the course of the ritual, the corpse was exhumed by the family and the skeleton cleaned of rotting flesh. The bones were then wrapped up as an effigy and placed in a cave. The colonial Dutch outlawed the practice because they considered it a health hazard, and the ritual no longer exists; the dead are now buried according to Islamic or Christian rites.

Voices from the past

Some of the objects here, while having no particular religious significance, tell much about the people and place where they originate. By its materials and carved motifs, the cooking spoon from the Moluccan island of Bacan on page 43 holds clues about the coastal environment there. The tortoiseshell comb, *hai kara jangga* (page 45), is associated with the local social customs of East Sumba. The comb is given by fathers to their daughters at puberty. Unmarried girls wear the comb inserted in the hair above their fringe to show that they are of marriageable age. Married women of the nobility also wear these combs. While *hai kara jangga* are not thought of as sacred objects or bride-price, the symbolic motifs carved on them imbue these objects with ideas about the supernatural world.

As items of a museum collection, all these objects hold the power to teach us about the people who inhabited specific forms of society, and thereby to deepen our understanding of human experience in the past and the present.

BULL-RACING SLEDGE ORNAMENT (*KALELES*)
This sledge ornament from Bangkalan, Madura
measures 375 x 177 cm and was acquired in 1938.
Inv. No: 23202

The kaleles *has its origins in the common
plough used to till rice fields.*

GRAVE MARKERS (*NISAN*)

Origin: Buton, Southeast Sulawesi
Size: 22 x 17 x 150 cm
Inv. No: 16526
Acquired: 1902

Two wooden grave markers carved with lotus leaf, flower, circle, and geometric motifs. Stylised platform houses appear on both markers. The pair of figures atop a four-legged animal (left marker) represents the ancestors riding into the afterworld; below, four figures stand on a multi-storey platform house, indicating the 'spirit village' of the deceased.

Judging by the circular and geometric motifs, as well as the number of human figures (probably representing servants), these markers were most likely made for the graves of a prosperous, respected individual and his wife.

SPIRIT SHIP [OPPOSITE]

Origin: Batak Karo, North
           Sumatra
Size: 244 x 108.5 cm
Inv. No: 23625
Acquired: 1940

Spirit ships like this one were affixed to the rooftops of spirit houses (*geritan*) of the Batak Karo (Sembiring clan), as a symbol of the soul's journey through life and death. Normally the Batak buried their dead. After a certain period, sometimes several years, a second funerary rite (*nurun-nurun*) would be held. After the skeleton was exhumed, the skull would be stored in the spirit house.

STONE HEAD [ABOVE]
Origin: Timor, East Indonesia
Size: 42 x 35 x 16 cm
Inv. No: 19321
Acquired: 1931

Sculpture of a head carved from
tuff—a form of volcanic rock—
and decorated with incised images
of a rooster, a gecko, and a
scorpion. These animals are
generally believed to symbolise life
in the afterworld and to be
effective in fending off harm. The
rooster motif is associated with the
sun, and thereby with strength,
courage, and fertility. The gecko
and the scorpion are associated
with water and the underworld.
The crest-shaped hairstyle is a type
of *sanggul*, or knot, typical to
Timor. This statue, which was
found in Timor, would have been
placed on top of a pile of stones
surrounding a sacred tree.

ANCESTRAL STATUES (*HAMPATONG*)
Origin: Central Kalimantan
Size: 315 and 318 cm high
Inv. Nos: 7534, 7536
Acquired: 1940

These statues are carved from a single piece of ironwood. The male holds a sword in front of himself in self-protection. The female carries a betelnut box, a pan-Indonesian symbol of hospitality and friendship.

The statues represent deceased individuals or more generalised ancestor figures, and also serve as guardian effigies to protect the community from disease and malevolent spirits. They would normally be placed at the entrance to the village, at the river's edge, or in front of the village longhouse. Among the Ngaju, the *hampatong* are placed inside the house and are believed to bring the family good fortune, health, and an abundant harvest.

BRIDAL VESSEL [OPPOSITE]
Origin: Lampung, Sumatra
Size: 40 cm high
Inv. No: 586
Acquired: 1885

An earthenware *kendi*, or drinking vessel, from the Tulang Bawang kingdom of Lampung. The porous nature of the clay keeps the water inside perpetually cool. *Kendi* are also used as containers for herbal tinctures and magical concoctions, and they serve as ritual objects in wedding ceremonies, where they are considered a symbol of marital longevity. The ceremonially dressed figure indicates that the vessel was used for wedding ceremonies. The water it contained would have been considered sacred and refreshing, embodying the concept of an ideal marriage.

CEREMONIAL HAT (*EJA PAKO, EPAKU*) [RIGHT]
Origin: Enggano Island, Sumatra
Size: 17.5 cm high; diam. 11.5 cm
Inv. No: 4082c
Acquired: 1855

A ceremonial hat of wood, embellished with feathers and a tin frog, worn by unmarried Enggano girls during the harvest feast of Kalea. The frog is thought to be an ancestor figure and a symbol of fertility.

SPIRIT EFFIGY [CENTRE]
Origin: Central Sulawesi
Size: 87 cm high
Inv. No: 16652
Acquired: 1920

This figure is a reproduction of those used in secondary burial rituals among ethnic groups living in the Lake Poso area. It is carrying a sheaf of rice.

BEADED BETELNUT BOX (*KAWILA*)
Origin: Sangir Talaud, North Sulawesi
Size: 26.5 x 16.5 x 11.7 cm
Inv. No: 21121
Acquired: 1935

A lontar palm-leaf box studded with coloured beads.

BRIDAL FIGURES
Origin: Takalar, South Sulawesi
Size: 13.5 cm high
Inv. No: 27161
Acquired: 1954

This earthenware joined statue
would have been part of wedding
rituals. The figures sit on a bridal
sofa; primary attention is paid to
the hairstyle and ornamentation.

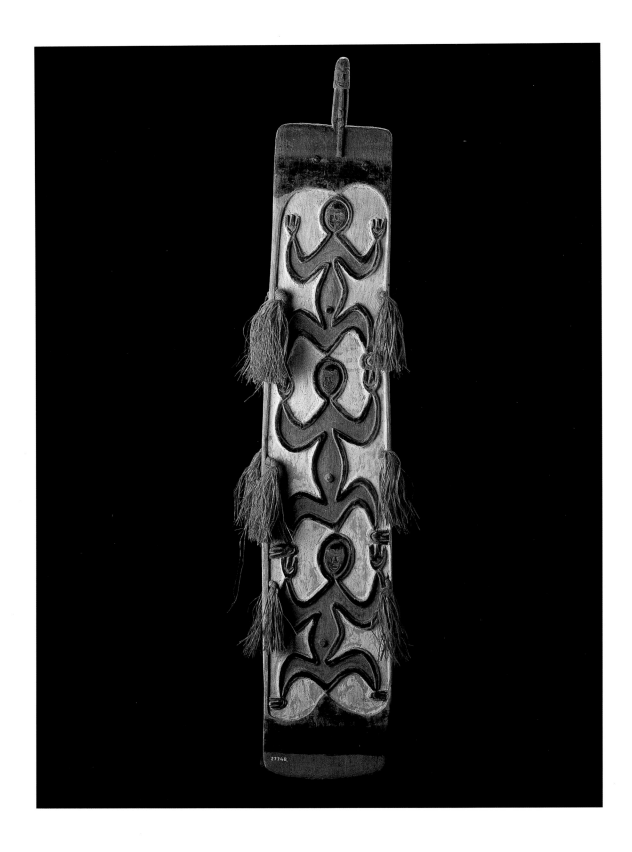

ASMAT SHIELD [OPPOSITE]
Origin: Irian Jaya (Asmat)
Size: 166.4 x 29.3 cm
Inv. No: 27746
Acquired: 1950

A mangrove wood shield used in both battle and ritual. The three figures represent kin spirits—father, mother, and grandfather.

HEAD REST [ABOVE]
Origin: Irian Jaya
Size: 69 x 21 x 7 cm
Inv. No: 26862
Acquired: 1930

A wooden and rattan head rest. At either end is the head of a crocodile biting a monkey. Bed pillows of this sort would be found in men's ritual houses and are thought to be used only by men. The social life of Irian men traditionally centres around their ceremonial house. Among groups around Cendrawasih Bay, the pillow is used as bride-price.

BEADED SKIRT (*SIREUW*) [RIGHT]
Origin: Irian Jaya
Size: 67 x 57 cm
Inv. No: 28696
Acquired: 1981

This skirt is worn by women, fastened on like an apron, during ceremonies connected with the felling of trees. The earliest beads in Irian Jaya were made of materials that were easy to bore, such as animal bones and wood.

RATTAN CHEST PROTECTOR
Origin: Wisselman, Irian Jaya
Size: 52.5 x 35 cm
Inv. No: 27672
Acquired: 1964

Rattan bark armour of this sort is not only worn to protect the torso in battle but is also used as part of victory rituals and in honouring war heroes.

War among these tribes is considered a sacred duty required by their ancestors; when there is no war, all aspects of life deteriorate, including farming, hunting, and trade.

TATOO INKWELL (*TUTANG*) [ABOVE]
Origin: Dayak, Central Kalimantan
Size: 21 x 6 x 8.5 cm
Inv. No: 7669
Acquired: 1886

A wooden receptacle carved in the form of a dog with a dragon's head, called an *aso*. This motif represents a goddess greatly feared by Dayaks. For many of the tribes of Central Kalimantan, tattooing is intimately tied to religious beliefs.

RICE HARVESTING KNIFE (*APAN-APAN*)
Origin: Dayak, South Kalimantan
Size: 14.9 x 16.9 cm
Inv. No: 20243
Acquired: 1932

The ironwood handle of this Dayak knife is carved with dragon motifs. At its centre is a length of bamboo, and on its underside a thin iron blade. In Dayak culture, the dragon motif is a symbol of the 'physical' world and a source of fertility, used in honouring the rice goddess. Rice plants are believed to possess an easily offended spirit that must be carefully protected during growth from evil influences that bring disease and pests.

COCONUT SHELL SPOON [ABOVE]
Origin: Bacan Island, North Maluku
Size: 63.5 cm long
Inv. No: 18858
Gift of Ph. Coolhaas, 1924

This spoon is made from half a coconut shell, with a wooden handle carved in the form of a snake entwining its length and biting a monkey at the tip. It was used as a cooking tool, not as a ritual object. Its rounded scoop would have been used in preparing sago. It was donated by the Dutch Controller at Laboeha on Bacan.

MUSICAL INSTRUMENT (*HAPE*)
Origin: Dayak, East Kalimantan
Size: 109.5 x 22 x 66 cm
Inv. No: 7622
Acquired: 1886

A two-stringed musical instrument made of wood with strings of rattan fibre; the head is decorated with an *aso* motif. The body has a full human figure motif, symbolising a god of the upperworld, or an ancestral guardian figure. The *aso* head signifies an entreaty for fertility and protection.

The *hape* is played at harvest rituals, with gongs, drums, and flutes, to accompany the *hudoq*, a group mask dance in which both men and women participate. The dancers wear strips of banana leaves fastened to the body from neck to foot. These represent the skin of a crocodile, to illustrate a theme of the dance.

— 43 —

Prow ornament (*Kora*)

Origin: Tanimbar Island,
Central Maluku
Size: 125 x 50 x 10.5 cm
Inv. No: 14308
Acquired: 1910

This prow ornament is carved out of ironwood. On its lower section is a creature resembling a fierce monitor lizard. Toward the front is carved a length of coiled rope and seashells. The spirals represent the ocean's waves. Monitor lizards, like the shark, symbolise the force of hostility and the hunt. The monitor lizard motif is associated with the underworld.

Prow ornaments serve as expressions of prosperity. They were also used as a standard for bearing home the head of a vanquished enemy. Seafarers on the islands of Aru, Kei, and Tanimbar ascribe human qualities to their boats, with male and female elements that combine in the boat's building process. In human beings, the 'life force' radiates from body and soul. For a boat, body and soul are associated with the hull and the prow ornament, rigging, and sail.

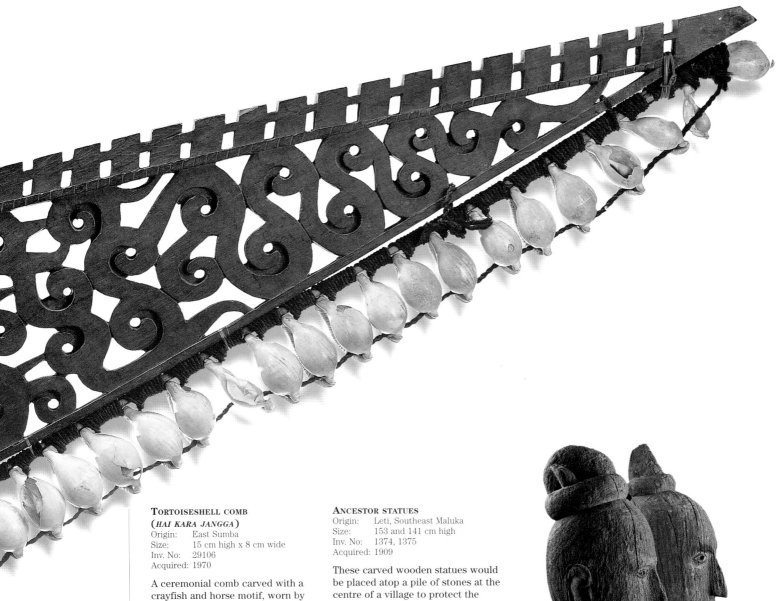

TORTOISESHELL COMB
(*HAI KARA JANGGA*)
Origin: East Sumba
Size: 15 cm high x 8 cm wide
Inv. No: 29106
Acquired: 1970

A ceremonial comb carved with a
crayfish and horse motif, worn by
East Sumbanese girls and women.

ANCESTOR STATUES
Origin: Leti, Southeast Maluka
Size: 153 and 141 cm high
Inv. No: 1374, 1375
Acquired: 1909

These carved wooden statues would
be placed atop a pile of stones at the
centre of a village to protect the
villagers from physical and
supernatural harm. The souls of the
deceased would be housed in a shrine,
there to be honoured by their
descendants and the community.
According to Leti belief, this
veneration formed part of the
devotional rites to Uperlu and
Upunusa, the sun god and earth
goddess. The effigies are also the
objects of rituals for requesting rain
and a good harvest.

    In ancient Indonesian art, the
human figure had two, perhaps
related, meanings: as guardian
figures and as a symbol of
ancestral spirits.

WINGED LION [OPPOSITE]
Origin: Klungkung, Bali
Size: 48 wide x 40 cm depth
Inv. No: 20856
Acquired: 1934

In Bali, a statue of a winged lion is often placed high inside the roof of a house at the joining of the beams. It acts as a symbolic protector to fend off spirits that might disturb the inhabitants. This particular statue, carved of wood and very finely painted, was located in the Kerta Ghosa (palace of justice) in Klungkung, in a pavilion that functioned as a court of customary law.

The winged lion recalls the Sutasoma legend, which tells of the life of the Buddha. It relates specifically to Sutasoma's overcoming an elephant-headed monster, a snake, and a lion.

WOODEN WALL DECORATION
Origin: Cirebon, West Java
Size: 68 x 42.5 cm
Inv. No: 22254
Acquired: 1938

This wooden wall ornament would be hung on a wall near the front door of a house as protection from untoward influences. The golden wayang figure is a variant of Batara Gana—the Hindu elephant god Ganesha—while the elephant standing on red clouds is reminiscent of South China's decorative art from the Ming Dynasty. The cloud motif and bright colours are of Chinese influence. Arabic script appears in the elephant's hair and lower trunk, an indication of Islamic culture. Cirebon, one of the oldest cities in Java, is characterised by a culture that combines elements of the Hindu, Chinese, and Islamic cultures. This ornament is a fine illustration of its eclectic nature.

GAMELAN ('SUKA RAME')
[OPPOSITE AND RIGHT]
Origin: Banten, West Java
Inv. Nos: 1243-1256 (69 pieces)
Acquired: 1941

The instruments are of bronze, set
in wooden frames carved with
vine, flower, and bird motifs.
The orchestra is called 'Suka
Rame', loosely translated as 'loves
a crowd'. The Banten were a
people who inhabited the western
portion of present-day West
Java province.

GAMELAN ('BANJARMASIN')
[ABOVE]
Origin: Banjarmasin, Kalimantan
Inv. No: 2572 (37 pieces)
Acquired: 1861.

A set of gamelan instruments from
the Banjarmasin kingdom in
(present-day) South Kalimantan.
This set includes a gong larger than
any found in a Javanese gamelan.
The orchestral pieces were made in
Surabaya, East Java and brought to
Kalimantan sometime during the
Banjarmasin reign.

CHAPTER 2

STONE

Hurled as a weapon, shaped to form a tool, erected as a monument, or carved to embody an idea—stone can be the most basic or the most sophisticated of materials.

The stone objects presented here tell a story about the rise of civilisation in the Indonesian archipelago. The earliest items date from the Neolithic era; but Indonesian peoples were making objects from stone much earlier than this. Paleolithic implements dating from the Pleistocene era have been found throughout the archipelago. Prehistoric man left behind a variety of material culture, ranging in form from the very simple to the complex.

This is apparent in objects found in various parts of Indonesia, such as axes, cutting blades, adzes, tools made from bone and horn, and various kinds of stone sarcophagi. They indicate stages of societal development and prehistoric culture referred to as the Hunter-Gatherer era, the Incipient Agriculture era, and the Bronze-and-Iron era.

Hunter-gatherers made great use of stone, bone and animal horn, and seashell to make hand-held adzes, cutting tools, spoons, and spearheads. In the first phase of the hunter-gatherer era, people were still nomadic; in a later phase they lived in caves or along the shores of lakes and the sea.

During the incipient agricultural era, people still made use of stone; but they were more selective in their choice, using such semi-precious stones as agate, chalcedony, and jade, and their stone-working techniques were more advanced. They made smoothly polished adzes, axes, and ornaments that may have been used as burial provisions or as items for barter. In this era, they also began to make earthenware objects. It is obvious that the objects these people made from animal and forest products—such as bone, leather, wood, rattan, bark, or bamboo—surely could not survive unless in fossil form.

Stone in worship

The incipient agricultural era saw the rise of the megalithic tradition in which large stones were the focus of worship. These objects include menhir, dolmen, and sarcophagi. Dolmen, menhir, and terraced monuments are classified as Old Megalithic, while stone sarcophagi, megalithic statues, and stone vessels are classified as New Megalithic, although in reality there was often a crossing over between elements of Old and New Megalithic.

To modern eyes, megalithic statues appear to be abstractions of ideas rather than realistic depictions. Facial features are simplified, and anatomy is very elementary or shown with altered, unrealistic proportions. In prehistoric art, the human form generally signifies important ancestral deities.

Concepts of ancestor worship established in prehistoric society persisted into the classical era up to the introduction of Islam; and this megalithic tradition, particularly in statuary, continues to exist in various regions in Indonesia, such as Nias, Toraja, Flores, and Sumba.

The influence of India

With the rise of the Hindu-Buddhist culture that once flourished in Indonesia, the iconography of statues changed dramatically, displaying influences deriving from India. The discovery of 5th century AD inscriptions in the area of Kutai clearly shows the presence of Indian culture in Indonesia: the beginnings of Pallawa script and a knowledge of Sanskrit, as well as indicators of a religion oriented to Hinduism.

Some Indian texts give precise indications for the construction of temples, and prescribe in detail the characteristics and placement of statues of deities. Because a statue was meant to be a 'vehicle' for the god, and the ornamentation an expression of its attributes, it was important not to violate this canon, although stylistic variation was allowed.

Assimilation

It seems clear from stone objects that remain—various inscriptions, literary works, and archeological artefacts in the form of temples and statuary—that Indian norms and rules for statuary were not simply swallowed whole, but absorbed into an underlying older Indonesian culture. No two temples in Indonesia have exactly the same form, for instance, and many display elements of the older megalithic culture. Statuary and decorative carving became freer in their treatment of the Indic Hindu gods, and the style became a purer expression of Indonesian experience. This 'local genius' becomes especially apparent in the 8th-15th century works of the Hindu-Buddhist kingdoms in Central and East Java, and reached its peak during the classical culture of Majapahit (1294-1527 AD).

The face of kingship

A significant deviation from the Indian code is a type of so-called portrait statue found in the Singasari-Majapahit period. These statues (an example is Ardhanari on page 69) were representations of deified kings, and they display both godly attributes and features emblematic of the dead (such as the flower held in both hands in front of the figure).

NANDI
This sculpture of Nandi came from Malang, East Java,
and dates back to the 13th century (Singasari).
Size: 120 x 90 x 30 cm; *Inv. No*: 324d;
date of acquisition unknown.

*Nandi is the divine bull who serves as the mount of
the god Shiva.*

STONE AXE [TOP RIGHT]
Material: Chalcedony
Origin: Cirebon, West Java
Size: 21 x 5.9 x 2.8 cm
Period: Neolithic
Inv. No: 4390
Acquired: 1938

The semi-precious material of this axe suggests that it was a ceremonial object, burial item or token of exchange. Axes of this sort made of common types of stone would have been fastened to a wooden handle with a sharp point to dig the soil, while the blade was used to chop wood.

SET OF BRACELETS, ROUGH TO FINE (WITH POLISHING TOOL, Inv. No: 5663**) [BELOW RIGHT]**
Material: Stone, chalcedony
Origin: Tasikmalaya, West Java
Period: Neolithic
Inv. Nos: 5679, 821, 4274, 4090
Acquired: 1933, 1941,1939, 1939

These objects show bracelets at various stages of fabrication.

STONE ADZE [BELOW]
Material: Chalcedony
Origin: Sukabumi, West Java
Size: 24.4 x 6.3 x 3.6 cm
Period: Neolithic
Inv. No: 5
Gift of Mr. E. Mundt, before 1880

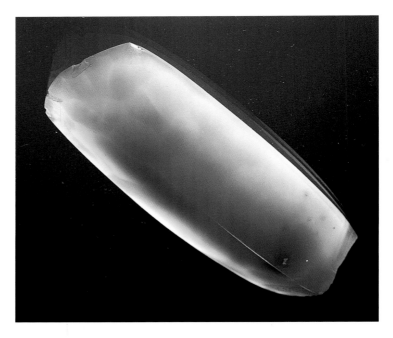

RECTANGULAR ADZE [OPPOSITE]
Material: Chalcedony
Size: 13 x 6.1 x 1.4 cm
Origin: Sukabumi, West Java
Period: Neolithic
Inv. No. :   7
Acquired: Before 1941

When semi-precious stones, like this chalcedony, are polished, the fine organic patterns within the stone become visible.

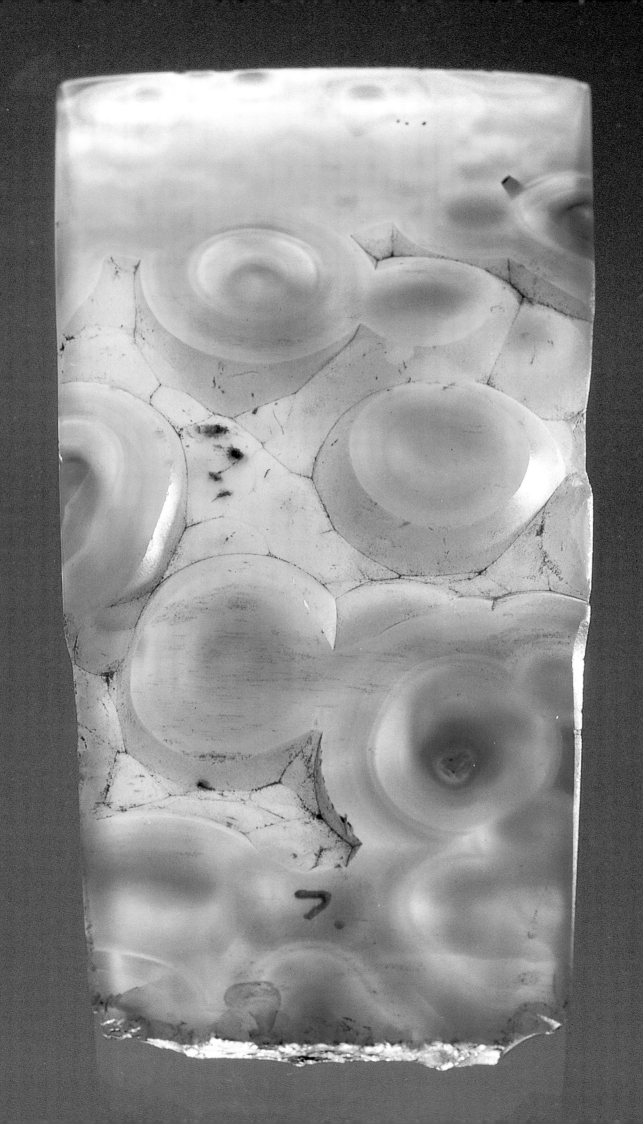

BRAHMA

Material: Stone
Origin: Wonosobo, Dieng, Central Java
Size: 90.5 x 30.5 x 31.7 cm
Period: 8th century
Inv. No: 6
Acquired: 1905

In the Hindu pantheon, Brahma is considered one of the supreme gods. He is the god of creation, described as *swayambhu* or 'born of himself'. He is identified by his four heads which face in the direction of the four winds, signifying the four Vedas, the four Yudas and the four Varna. Brahma is usually depicted riding on the shoulders of his mount, the goose Hangsa, who supports the god's feet in lotus blossoms held in each hand. In this representation, Hangsa is entirely anthropomorphic. The stiff angular style is characteristic of statuary produced by the Dieng civilisation; but Hangsa's face is lively and sweet. This piece is a good example of the freedom that Indonesian craftsmen exercised in regard to Indian rules of statuary.

PRASASTI HANTANG [OPPOSITE]

Material: Stone
Origin: Ngantang, East Java
Size: 173 cm high
Period: 1135
Inv. No: D.9
Acquired: date unknown

The face of this stele inscribed in Old Javanese script bears an emblem in the form of Narasimha, an incarnation of Vishnu. The inscription begins with *Pangjalu Jayati* ('Victorious Pangjalu'). Pangjalu is the name of a kingdom. It mentions that on the date 13 Krenapaksa in the month of Badrawada, of the Saka year 1057 (or September 7, 1135 AD), Sri Maharaja sang Mapanji Jayabhaya Sriwarmeswara Madhusudana-wataranidita Suhretsingha Parakrama Digjayottunngadewa reconfirmed that the village of Hantang was exempt from taxes, as had been previously granted by the king buried at Gayapada and Nagapuspa.

PRASASTI TELAGA BATU [RIGHT]

Material: Stone
Origin: Telaga Batu, Palembang, Sumatra
Size: 155 x 143 cm
Period: 6th-7th century (Sriwijaya)
Inv. No: D.155
Acquired: 1964

This stele is inscribed with 28 lines of text in Old Malay with Pallawa script which is very worn. It seems that an oath of loyalty was sworn by drinking water that streamed over the stone.

AGASTYA [LEFT]
Material: Stone
Origin: Banon, Magelang,
           Central Java
Size: 192 x 74 x 47 cm
Period: 8th century
Inv. No: 63b
Acquired: 1905

This statue of Agastya, the divine sage (*resi*), shows him standing upright, wearing a long beard and moustache. Of the two figures kneeling in homage at the sage's feet, only fragments remain; they may have been disciples. His attributes include a rosary and the remains of what was most likely a *kendi*. Agastya is usually depicted with a protruding belly—signifying a store of knowledge.

GANESHA
Material: Stone
Origin: Banon, Central Java
Size: 148 cm high
Period: 8th century
Inv. No: 186b
Acquired: 1906

This statue of Ganesha, the elephant-headed son of Shiva and Parvati, shows him in *sitasana* position, sitting with the soles of his feet together. He holds an axe (*parasu*), a rosary (*aksamala*), and a cup from which he is savouring nectar with his trunk—this represents his unquenchable thirst for knowledge. His headdress shows the *candrakapala*, or skull-crescent motif, and he wears a caste cord in the form of a snake.

Ganesha is revered as the god who eradicates danger; statues of him are often found at the confluence of two rivers or the edges of cliffs. Ganesha is also considered to be the god of prudence and diplomacy.

BOROBUDUR BUDDHA

Material: Stone
Origin: Borobudur, Central Java
Size: 123 cm high
Period: 8th-9th century
Inv. No: 227
Acquired: 1951

By the 19th century, the great
Central Javanese Buddhist temple
of Borobudur had become a ruin. It
was restored in the 1980s and is
once again a place of religious
ceremonial practice.

SHIVA AND PARVATI
Material: Stone
Origin: Klaten, Central Java
Size: 198 x 48 x 52 cm
Period: 8th - 9th century AD
Inv. No: 6091
Acquired: 1935

Shiva, sometimes described as 'The Destroyer', is the god of transformation. This statue depicts Shiva in his Uma-Sahita-Murti manifestation, that is, together with his consort, Uma/Parvati. The couple stands in the *samabhanga* position (erect with legs together) on a rectangular lotus pedestal. The figures are carved with great attention to the detail of their ornamentation, as required by the Indian canon of religious statuary.

KARTIKEYA [OPPOSITE ABOVE]
Material: Stone
Origin: Yogyakarta, Central Java
Size: 85 cm high
Period: 10th century
Inv. No: 202
Acquired: 1877

The god of war, shown riding his
mount, the peacock. His right hand
holds a flower.

KUVERA [OPPOSITE BELOW]
Material: Stone
Origin: Yogyakarta, Central Java
Size: 128 cm high
Period: 9th-10th century
Inv. No: 207
Acquired: 1877

The Hindu god of wealth is usually
portrayed with a protruding belly.

DWARAPALA
Material: Stone
Origin: Central Java
Size: 105 cm high
Period: 9th-10th century
Inv. No: 210
Acquired: 1951

Dwarapala, typically of guardian
statuary, presents a frightening
grimace to fend off danger.
    In Java, Dwarapala statues were
always placed at the gate or
entrance door. At Candi Sewu in
Central Java, a hefty Dwarapala
with a snarling face stands at the
temple gate.

ADITYAVARMAN

Material: Stone
Origin: Padang Lawas, West Sumatra
Size: 4.41 m high
Period: 14th century
Inv. No: 4915
Acquired: date unknown

This monumental statue is in the form of a Bhairawa—a demonic being that embodies negative impulses. The figure is shown standing on a corpse atop a pile of skulls; he holds a sacrificial knife and a bowl in the form of a skull. It is thought to be a 'portrait statue' of the 14th-century Sumatran king Adityavarman.

Adityavarman was the son of a Javanese prince and a Sumatran princess who had been captured during the defeat of Malayu by East Java in 1260. Adityavarman was sent to Sumatra, probably as a Majapahit viceroy; but apparently he broke with his parental court and set up a kingdom of his own in the highlands of western Sumatra—an area thought to be rich in gold and rice cultivation. There he attempted to impose a Javanese-style court society among the egalitarian matrilineal Minangkabau people. Adityavarman left some 30 inscriptions throughout Sumatra and Java, from which one concludes that he belonged to an esoteric Buddhist sect that practised the overcoming of negative impulses by indulging in them. After Adityavarman's death, his kingdom seems to have disappeared.

CANDI PULO RELIEFS

Material: Stone
Origin: Padang Lawas, West Sumatra
Size: 52 x 36 cm
Period: 13th-14th century
Inv. No: 6120, 6121
Acquired: 1925

Candi Pulo was one of the
numerous elaborate brick shrines
built by an esoteric Buddhist sect
on the Padang Lawas plain.
'Padang Lawas', which means 'wide
plain', lies between the two
mountain ranges that run the
length of Sumatra, and it is here
that the huge statue of
Adityavarman [opposite] was
found. The cult seems to have
practised a variant of Vajrayana
Buddhism, and there are
indications that it was allied to
sects in Nepal and Sri Lanka.

HAYAGRIVA

Material: Stone
Origin: Candi Jago, Tumpang,
 Malang, East Java
Size: 141 x 75.5 x 56 cm
Period: 13th century (Singasari)
Inv. No: 76a (3622)
Acquired: 1893

Hayagriva is worshipped as the
god of knowledge. Here he is
depicted as demonic; his crown
bears a serpent and a diadem of
skulls, and he wears a caste cord
in the form of a snake. His
consort (not shown here) is the
fearsome Bhrkuti.

*The two Buddhist statues on this
page are from the Hindu-Buddhist
temple Candi Jago. They form
part of a mandala of four around
the bodhisattva Amoghapasa.*

SYAMATARA

Material: Stone
Origin: Candi Jago, Tumpang,
 Malang, Central Java
Size: 198 cm high
Period: 13th century
Inv. No: 112a
Acquired: 1893

Syamatara is the consort of
Sudhanakumara, the gentler of the
two bodhisattva couples attending
Amoghapasa at Candi Jago.

MUKHA LINGGA
Material: Stone
Origin: Singasari, East Java
Size: 64 x 26 x 12.4 cm
Period: 1361
Inv. No: 352/ D.89
Acquired: date unknown

The bottom of this Shivite
monolith is squared and very
rough, indicating that it was placed
in the ground or in another object.
The upper part is octagonal with a
rounded top. The face (*mukha*) is a
kala head with splayed hands.
Above the head is written (in
numerals) the Saka year 1283, or
1361 AD. The *kala* figure is often
carved above temple gateways in
present-day Hindu Bali, where it is
also called a *bhoma*.

NARASIMHA
Material: Stone
Origin: Tulungagung, East Java
Size: 49 x 125 cm
Period: c. 11th-13th century
Inv. No: 21
Acquired: date unknown

Narasimha is one of the
incarnations of Vishnu during his
war against Hiranyakasipu. When
the heavens were about to be
attacked by Asura Hiranyakasipu,
the gods asked Vishnu to help
them. During the battle, Vishnu
transformed himself into a lion-
headed creature and tore
Hiranyakasipu to pieces.

PRAJÑAPARAMITA

Material: Stone
Origin: Malang, East Java
Size: 126 cm high
Period: 13th century (Singasari)
Inv. Nos: 1403/1387
Acquired: 1923

Prajñaparamita, goddess of wisdom, is seen here seated in the *vajrasana* posture on a lotus pedestal. Her hands are raised in the turning-of-the-wheel-of-law pose (*dharmacakramudra*). On the stele above a relief carving of a lotus blossom is a book, the *Prajñaparamita Sutra*.

Prajñaparamita is a goddess of high standing in Mahayana Tantric Buddhism; she is considered the *sakti*, or consort, of the highest Buddha (in the Buddhist pantheon known as Vajradhara); she symbolises perfect knowledge. As with many statues from East Java, this one is thought to be the 'portrait statue' of a queen, possibly Ken Dedes, the infamously beautiful wife of the first raja of Singasari, Ken Angrok.

PARVATI

Material:	Stone
Origin:	Candi Rimbi, near Majawarna, Jombang, East Java
Size:	190 cm high
Period:	Majapahit (14th century)
Inv. No:	256a/103b (2971)
Acquired:	1869

This statue of Parvati (the consort of Shiva) is thought to also represent a Majapahit queen, the consort of the king Krtarajasa Jayawardhana. There are striking similarities between this statue and the androgynous Ardhanari statue (opposite).

While many believe that both statues are from the same *candi* and represent husband and wife, there is evidence that the Krtarajasa statue was originally at Candi Sumberjati. The Parvati was found at Candi Rimbi.

The *Nagarakrtagama*, a long poem glorifying the reign of Rajasanagara (Hayam Wuruk), mentions the inauguration of a posthumous statue of the king's grandmother. This lady, the Rajapatni Gayatri and consort of Krtarajasa, was the daughter of the last Singasari king, Kertanagara. Indeed, Krtarajasa married four of the king's daughters. With Gayatri, Krtarajasa had a daughter, Tribhuwana, with whom the Parvati statue has also been identified. At one time, Tribhuwana ruled in the name of her mother, who had taken holy orders after the death of Krtarajasa in 1309—and thus was also a Majapahit queen. In 1329 or 1330, Tribhuwana married a nobleman and in 1334 bore him a son, Hayam Wuruk, who became king upon the death of his grandmother, the Rajapatni, in 1350.

Although the iconography of the Parvati and Ardhanari statues is very similar, the sculptor's hand is not the same. The Parvati is fuller and softer, and yet more formally balanced; the proportions are the idealisation of a human reality; and the carving is more detailed. The Ardhanari statue, in comparison, is more stylised and austere, suggesting an earlier period.

WATER SPOUT [ABOVE]
Material: Stone
Origin: Mojokerto, East Java
Size: 67 cm high
Period: 10th-11th century
Inv. No: 309
Acquired: 1939

A good example of the suppleness
of Majapahit sculpture.

ARDHANARI
Material: Stone
Origin: Surabaya, East Java
Size: 143 x 67 x 55 cm
Period: 14th century
Inv. No: 104a
Acquired: 1893

Ardhanari is a manifestation of
Shiva in unity with his consort,
Parvati. This Ardhanari is thought
to be a 'portrait statue' of the first
Majapahit king, Krtarajasa. The
figure's divinity is indicated by his
four arms and the attributes he
holds, such as the lotus and the
three-pronged weapon *trisula*.

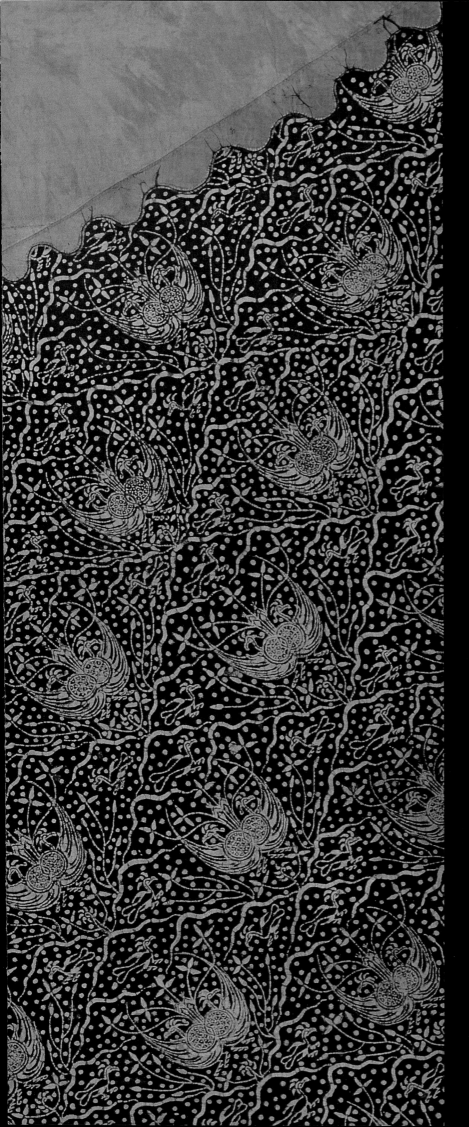

CHAPTER 3

TEXTILES

The weaving and patterning of cloth is an intimate art, carried out mostly by women; it is cloth that stands between a person and the world. In Indonesia, textiles serve not only socially, as garments and signifiers, but also metaphysically, as objects of ritual power. The grandeur of Indonesia's textile tradition arises from the great variety of its ethnic groups, whose distinctive cultures are most vividly revealed in their various textiles. By studying the function of different kinds of cloth, their design motifs, and the regard in which they are held by the people who make and use them, one can learn much about the way different people think and live. Textiles also hold clues about the physical and technological environment in which they are made. The fibres and dyes may come from local plants. Techniques and design motifs may reflect a history of isolated development or of association with distant cultures.

Traditional garments in Indonesia are mostly wrapped or draped rather than sewn. They consist of rectangular cloths of four main sorts: the *kain*, worn around the hips and legs; the *sarong*, in which smaller *kain* are sewn together in a tube-like garment; the *selimut*, a large blanket-like cloth worn as a mantle; and the versatile *selendang*, a long, broad sash that may be wrapped around the torso, tied as a headcloth or draped over one shoulder, sometimes tied in a sling to carry a child.

While clothing is structurally simple, the graphic language of design motifs found in Indonesia is especially complex. Among the most ancient design motifs are geometric patterns thought to have originated with what is known as the Dongson bronze culture that descended from northern Vietnam around 3,000 years ago and whose influence was felt in the Indonesian archipelago for many centuries after Dongson itself died out. These motifs—single and interlocking spirals, hooks, and triangles, as well as stylised anthropomorphic figures associated with ancestor veneration—are found on textiles across the Indonesian archipelago, from Sumatra to Irian Jaya. Among these abstract designs, one of the most prevalent is the narrow isosceles triangle called the *tumpal*. The *tumpal* motif is associated with the sacred mountain (*meru*)—the abode of the gods and ancestors, where one undergoes self-purification and communicates with the spiritual world. The mountain is an image deep in the psyche of people who live in a highly volcanic environment, and this motif recurs in the art adorning Javanese-Balinese structures.

Exclusive motifs

A very different and particularly restricted design motif is the lyrically figurative genre called *semen*, where all manner of natural and mythical creation is represented, from plants and animals to dragons and clouds. The word *semen* comes from the Javanese '*semi*', meaning 'to grow'. In *semen*, a number of symbolically potent motifs are assembled to form an over-all repeating pattern: the *meru*, sacred dwelling place of the gods; birds, a symbol of the upper world; the throne (*singasana*), seat of just, protective power; flames (*modang*), the symbol of supernatural power; wings (*lar* or *sawat*), symbolising the crown; tendrils and flowers, indicating the middle world of life; and so on. It is in the larger pattern that these motifs begin to convey messages specific to Javanese culture. For instance, the family of a betrothed girl wears batik with the *semen rante* motif (*rante*, or chain, symbolising a close and binding relationship). *Semen* patterns are also worn by nobility as a way of expressing their position in the royal hierarchy.

The role of textiles in Indonesian societies remains important even today. Textiles may signal distinctions of rank (as in the sacred *batik dodot* of the royal families of Central Java, and the *songket selendang* of West Sumatra); some are essential to ritual (for example, the *geringsing* cloth of Bali, or the *pakiri mbola* of Sumba). The 'ship cloth' from Lampung, Sumatra is used in ceremonies throughout a person's life cycle. Nearly all the textiles presented here are felt by the people who use them to embody supernatural qualities.

Weaving and dyeing

Indonesian textiles generally fall into two broad categories of technique for creating design motifs—*ikat* weaving and batik. Both entail resist-dyeing, where the distribution of colour is controlled by isolating certain areas. In *ikat*, the pattern is dyed into the threads before weaving (either the warp or the weft, except in the case of the very rare double *ikat*, in which the pattern is dyed into both). The *songket* technique is a variation of this in which designs are applied with a supplementary weft or warp in another material, often threads of gold or silver. In batik, a design is worked upon plain cloth by inscribing the pattern in wax. This may be done by drawing directly with hot wax, or by means of a copper stencil. Pattern and colour are gradually built up through repeated processes of applying wax and dye. Other less widely found techniques of resist-dyeing are *pelangi*—a form of tie-dyeing—and *teritik*, where the resist pattern is created with stitched thread. Although *ikat* and batik are not unique to Indonesia, they have achieved a level of technical virtuosity here that have made Indonesian textiles highly prized by international collectors.

For Indonesians themselves, it is not the complex beauty of their textiles that makes them treasures, but their deep cultural significance. As individual pieces, each of those shown here represents detailed ideas about human identity within a particular society. As part of a collection, textiles provide a survey of the social, spiritual, and artistic wealth of the Indonesian nation.

KAIN DODOT
This textile came from Yogyakarta, Central Java
and measures 115 x 375 cm.
Inv. No: 23150; *acquired*: 1938.

A batik prada *ceremonial cloth whose use was
reserved exclusively for the nobility.*

BEADED *SARONG* (*LAU HADA*)

Origin: East Sumba,
          Eastern Indonesia
Size: 150 x 125 cm
Inv. No: 3446
Acquired: 1886

A *sarong* or hip cloth sewn from several panels of cloth woven from heavy *kapok* thread. The base colours of brown and black are from natural dyes. Typical sources included indigo (*tarum*), tumeric (*kunyit*), candlenut (*kemiri*), and mud (*lumpur*). The figurative motifs have been sewn on with beads and cowrie shells, a symbol of fertility, power, and prestige. This type of sarong is also called *pakiri mbola*, loosely translated as 'dowry chest', and is greatly valued by the Sumbanese. It is worn by women of the nobility during ceremonies.

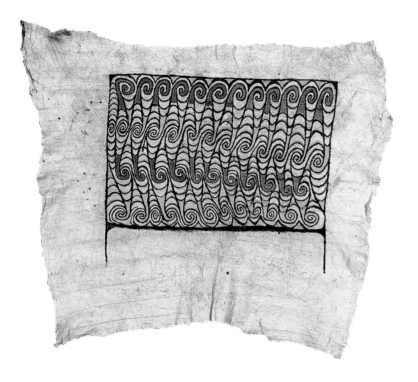

SHROUD [LEFT]
Origin: Sentani, Irian Jaya
Size: 144 x 132 cm
Inv. No: 24171
Gift of Mr. J. Hoog Land, 1940

A bark cloth shroud would have been hung over the grave of a tribal leader after having been used to wrap the corpse. This Dongson-style motif of interlocking spirals is often seen in Sentani art.

CEREMONIAL COAT (*LEMBA*)
Origin: Toraja, South Sulawesi
Size: 59 x 99 cm
Inv. No: 16875
Acquired: 1936

A dress made of un-dyed bark cloth painted with motifs of stylised buffalo heads, symbolic of the fertile earth. The shape of the buffalo horn is equated with the crescent moon; and it is thought that the dead are conveyed into the afterlife on buffaloes.

Bark cloth garments are called *fuya* in Central Sulawesi. The coat shown here would be worn with a layered bark cloth skirt—an outfit that somewhat resembles Portuguese costumes of the 16th century.

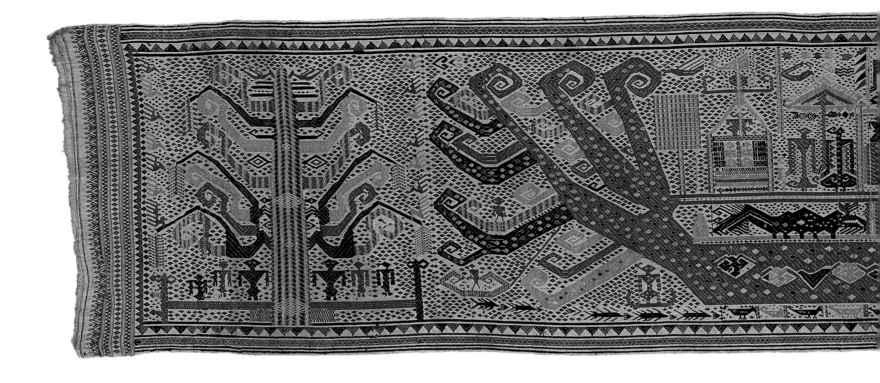

SHIP CLOTH (*PALEPAI*)

Origin: Lampung, Sumatra
Size: 282 x 61 cm
Inv. No: 26546
Acquired: 1949

This long *palepai* is of cotton interwoven with a supplementary weft of coloured threads. The ceremonial motif is a ship carrying both human and four-legged passengers, a ceremonial parasol, and a tree.

Palepai were made in the region of Paminggir, near Semangka and Teluk Lampung in South Sumatra. Since the 1950s, production of these ceremonial cloths has virtually ceased, and they have become extremely rare.

The motif of human figures symbolises the oldest male, who inherits the ship cloth passed down from generation to generation. The tree motif is called *pohon hayat* or *kayu ara*, meaning 'tree of life', an element common to both Hinduism and Islam. Four-legged creatures are a symbol of the lower world; the ship represents the human life cycle and the passage from each stage of life to the next. The *palepai* was hung on a wall during rites of passage for the noblity.

DOUBLE *IKAT* (*GERINGSING PATELIKUR ISI*)

Origin: Tenganan, South Bali
Size: 212 x 42.5 cm
Inv. No: 20215
Acquired: 1932

In Southeast Asia, the very rare double-*ikat* cloth is woven only in the village of Tenganan Pegeringsingan, Bali—hence this textile is known as *geringsing* cloth. In this difficult technique, the pattern is first dyed into both the warp and weft threads, a process that can take several months. In the weaving process, the warp and weft threads must meet exactly in order to form the pattern. The colours typical of *geringsing* are a muted palette of natural dyes. Before dyeing, the threads are soaked in a bath of candlenut (*kemiri*) oil, wood ash, and lye. Then the pattern is dyed, first in indigo, followed by a red dye from the root of the bengkudu tree. The characteristic rust brown is the result of layering red over indigo.

Geringsing woven with motifs from the wayang repertory are especially prized and serve many ritual functions—as burial shrouds, as covers for temple shrines, and as 'medicine' in treating scorpion bites.

Tenganan is remarkable for the ancient orthodoxy of its culture. It is considered to be 'Bali Aga', a term for pre-Majapahit Balinese culture, but in some respects it is unlike any other village on the island: to this day, for instance, villagers must marry within the village or live outside its walls.

SARONG BENTENAN [OPPOSITE]
Origin: Minahasa, North Sulawesi
Size: 67 x 82 cm
Inv. No: 2766
Acquired: 1886

Kain Bentenan—a warp *ikat* that
until the 1880s was made only in
the region of Lake Bentenan—
displays motifs inspired by the silk
cinde cloth of India, a culture with
which the Minahasans were
familiar. A motif of diamonds,
triangles, and meanders, called
patola, is characteristic of cinde
cloth; among the Minahasans, the
word *patola* (from Patolu, Gujarat
in India) was synonymous with
Indian cloth.
    The difficult process of weaving
this cloth was accompanied by a
ritual. The final product was worn
by female priests during religious
ceremonies.

SASH (*SELENDANG*) [RIGHT AND BELOW]
Origin: Timor, East Indonesia
Size: 138 x 45 cm
Inv. No: 23257
Bequest of Mr. J. W. van Dapperen, 1938

A warp-*ikat* sash made with
natural dyes. Red was traditionally
the colour of garments worn in
battle; it symbolises bravery and
gallantry. This *selendang* was worn
as part of ceremonial dress.

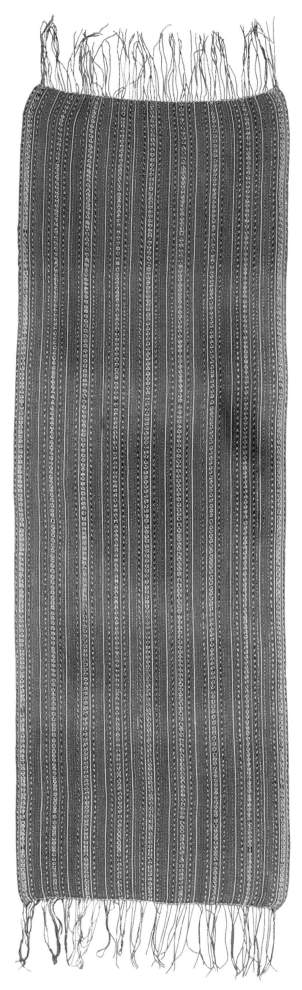

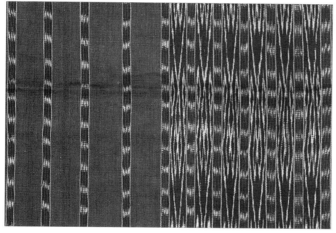

***SONGKET* SASH (*ULOS RAGI IDUP*)**
Origin: Batak Toba, North Sumatra
Size: 200 x 120 cm
Inv. No: 20333
Gift of Mr. Ir J. L. Moens, 1932

This cotton *ulos* displays a geometric motif called *ragi idup*, or 'pattern of life'. Until the mid-19th century, these cloths were worn by both men and women; men wrapped them around their waist, and women wore them from chest to waist. The Batak people believed that the *ulos* warmed the soul as well as the body, giving it strength and reviving the spirit. Red and white in the *ragi idup* is highly valued: it is considered sacred, providing strength and tranquillity in the face of hardship.

Ulos such as this one were a gift from women to men, with the intent of protecting the strength of the wearer. They were worn during rites of passage.

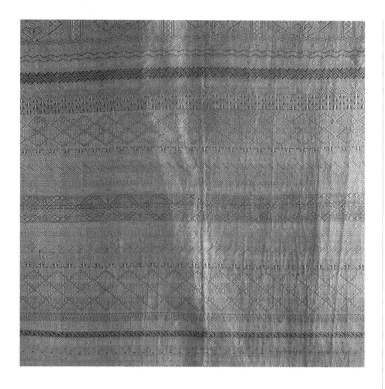

Songket is a brocade-weaving technique in which an ornamental pattern is woven with supplementary weft threads, usually of gold, silver or silk.

SONGKET SAMBAS (SARUNG SONGKET PETAK) [OPPOSITE]
Origin: Sambas, West Kalimantan
Size: 127 x 95 cm
Inv. No: 29107
Acquired: 1886

A *sarong* woven of cotton and gold thread. *Songket* cloth from Sambas features stylised geometrical and floral motifs. The Sambas are a branch of the Malay ethnic group. The kingdom of Sambas is believed to have been established by a Majapahit nobleman, Ratu Sepudek; during his reign, the influence of Islam spread rapidly. This type of *songket* was worn by both men and women during weddings and other ceremonies.

SONGKET PANDAI SIKUT (TENGKULUK) [ABOVE]
Origin: Padang Panjang, West Sumatra
Size: 170 x 140 cm
Inv. No: 21678
Gift of Dr. A. N. J. Th. van der Hoop, 1936

A ceremonial cloth of silk and gold thread. *Tengkuluk* is a kind of *selendang* or sash tied as a headdress. The Minangkabau women tie their distinctive headdresses with the ends tapered to resemble buffalo horns, like the roof-line of Minangkabau matrilineal clan houses.

WALL HANGING (DALEMSE) [BELOW]
Origin: Sangihe Talaud, North Sulawesi
Size: 115 x 22 cm
Inv. No: 27099
Acquired: 1953

This cloth is woven in the *songket* technique using a yarn made from the fibres of a plantain tree (*Musa textilis*). *Kapok* yarn is used for the supplementary weft. The result is a hardy, water-resistant type of cloth called *koffo* .

The Sangihe Talaud peoples use plantain yarn in the production of clothing, cloth, and sirih containers. Large *koffo* cloths were normally used as space dividers.

FLAG [OPPOSITE]
Origin: Banten, West Java
Size: 122 x 97 cm
Inv. No: 5602
Acquired: 1890

This flag was made with the batik resist-dye method and embellished with gold (*prada*) in images of Arabic script, a star, and a double-edge sword known as 'the sword of Hasan Husin, grandson of the Prophet Muhammad'. Carried into battle or during ritual displays of invulnerability (*debus*), it functioned more as a banner than a flag.

'PATCHWORK' BATIK (*KAIN TAMBAL*) [ABOVE]
Origin: Cirebon, West Java
Size: 260 x 103 cm
Inv. No: 20457
Acquired: 1933

The *tambal* or patchwork motif of triangular panels filled with patterns—some of Indian and Chinese influence, others old Javanese—reflects the syncretism that is distinctive of Cirebon art. Some believe that the motif was inspired by the clothing of the poor as a symbol of renunciation.

SIMBUT BATIK [RIGHT]
Origin: Banten, West Java
Size: 198 x 118 cm
Inv. No: 21164
Acquired: 1936

Simbut, which means 'blanket' in Sundanese, is an ancient type of cloth of the Baduy people. The pattern is drawn on the cloth with a paste made from glutinous rice. This *simbut* is ornamented with very old design motifs. It would have been worn during rituals surrounding birth and death and such rites of passage as circumcision. When placed over an object or person, the *simbut* also had a guardian function.

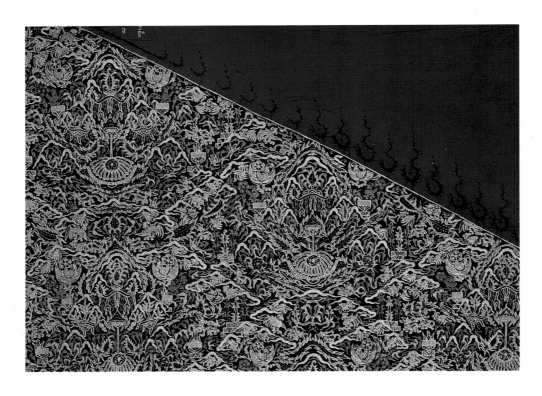

***DODOT* CLOTH [TOP AND OPPOSITE]**
Origin: Yogyakarta, Central Java
Size: 370 x 214 cm
Inv. No: 23146
Bequest of Mr. J.W. van Dapperen, 1938

***DODOT* CLOTH [BOTTOM]**
Origin: Yogyakarta, Central Java
Size: 382 x 226 cm
Inv. No: 23144
Bequest of Mr. J.W. van Dapperen, 1938

Dodot *are large batik cloths worn by the royalty and courtiers of the* kraton *of Central Java. The two shown here are both examples of* semen *patterns, enhanced by the application of gold in leaf or* powder form in a technique called prada. *In Solo and Yogyakarta,* prada *would have been applied only to sacred patterns, such as* kawung, *and to those restricted to the king's or sultan's immediate* family (such as parang rusak). Dodot prada *are considered sacred cloths and are worn only on ceremonial occasions such as weddings, or in costume for sacred dances.*

KAIN BATIK [TOP RIGHT]

Origin: Rembang, Central Java
Size: 260 x 104 cm
Inv. No: 273
Acquired: 1992

Made by Raden Agung Kartini
(1879-1904), a young Javanese
noblewoman who championed
women's emancipation.

KAIN BATIK [BOTTOM RIGHT]

Origin: Pamekasan, Madura
Size: 224 x 100 cm
Inv. No: 29100
Gift of Mrs. Faigah Ismail, Pamekasan,
1997

This batik *tulis* cloth is worked in
an old motif characteristic of
Pamekasan, known as *jagad kupu*,
or 'butterfly world'. Batik *jagad
kupu* and batik dyed in deep indigo
blue were generally worn only by
the nobility during ceremonies.

BATIK *PRADA*

Origin: Semarang, Central Java
Size: 217 x 102 cm
Inv. No: 15034
Acquired: 1912

A batik cloth enhanced by *prada*.
One end of the cloth has a *tumpal*
motif of slender isosceles triangles
containing zoomorphic figures,
flowers and tendrils. The body of
the cloth is filled with a repeating
diamond pattern (*belah ketupat*)
of stylised flowers.

   Batik *prada* was produced in
great quantity at workshops run
by Indonesian-born Chinese and
Eurasians because of strong
local demand.

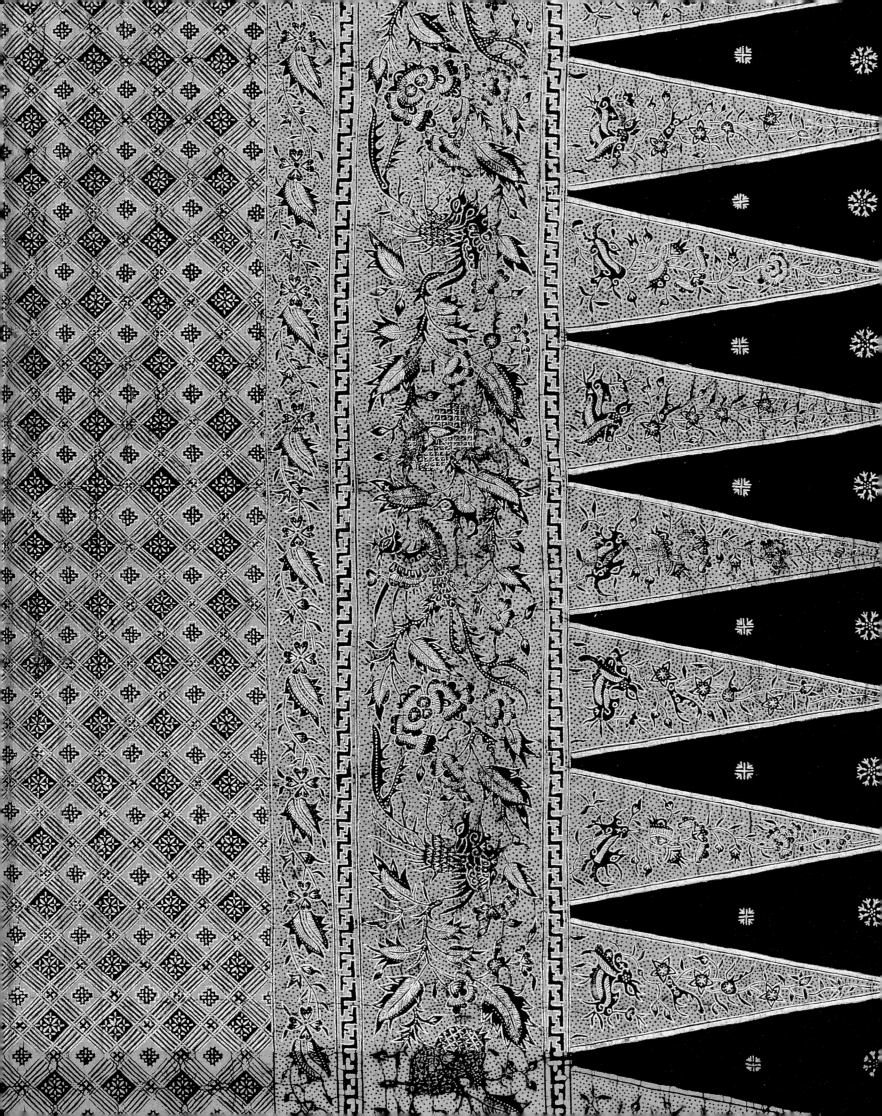

CHAPTER 4

CERAMICS

T he making of ceramics—objects of fired clay—is one of mankind's most ancient arts, as old as agriculture. The word 'ceramics' itself comes from the Greek *Keramikos*, the deity who protected potters, derived from *keramos*, or potter's earth. In Indonesia, ceramics appeared in the Neolithic era and is known to have flourished during the Bronze-and-Iron Age, perhaps even earlier, and the prehistoric traditions are still practised alongside modern techniques.

'Ceramics' embraces earthenware and terracotta (fired at temperatures ranging from 350C°-1,000C°), stoneware (fired at 1,150C°-1,300C°) and porcelain (fired at 1,250C°-1,350C°).

The ceramic process is essentially a matter of forming wet clay into the desired shape and subjecting it to heat under controlled conditions. The shape may be achieved by forming clay on a rotating wheel, by pressing it in a mould, or by shaping it directly by hand using a paddle and anvil. Extentions (such as handles and spouts) are added by binding two pieces with a thinner clay mixture called 'slip'. Decoration may be painted on, carved or stamped; or additional clay may be applied to the surface. Glazes are often applied in a second firing to impart strength, colour, and a more watertight surface.

Clues to the past

Most of the pieces presented in this chapter are foreign. They derive from an unusual collection amassed over 31 years and bequeathed to the National Museum by its collector, E.W. van Orsoy de Flines when he returned to his native Holland in 1959. The thesis of the collection was unique: foreign ceramics found in Indonesia would shed light on the history of ancient Indonesia, especially in regard to its relations with foreign countries. Besides their historical importance, many of these are treasures in their own right by virtue of their craftsmanship or rarity. The collection includes pieces from:

1. CHINA:

    a. Han Dynasty (205 BC-220)

    b. Tang Dynasty (618-906)

    c. Song Dynasty (960-1279)

    d. Yuan Dynasty (1279-1368)

    e. Ming Dynasty (1368-1644)

    f. Qing Dynasty (1644-1912)

2. VIETNAM (13th-16th century)

3. THAILAND (13th-16th century)

4. JAPAN (17th-19th century)

5. CAMBODIA (10th-14th century)

6. MYANMAR (11th-16th century)

7. EASTERN EUROPE (17th-18th century)

8. EUROPE (17th-18th century)

The importance of the foreign collection is apparent when one considers the strategic location of the Indonesian archipelago across the trade routes between India and China, the two great centres of ancient international trade. Indonesia became an object of interest to European traders in the 16th century when they discovered the wealth of spices there. The origin of foreign ceramics in Indonesia is closely related to trade, much of it as a medium of trade itself.

The exchange of goods

The usual type of trade carried on during this period was the exchange of agricultural produce, each country seeking items not available domestically. Chinese traders bought spices with tea, silk, and ceramics made in their own country. Although much of the foreign trade ceramics was of low quality, for everyday household use only, some of it was unusually fine. Occasionally ceramic items were made on order to the buyer's taste, such as ware decorated with Arabic script (an example is on page 106). If the ceramic quality was good, the piece would be kept as an heirloom.

A ceramic piece might also enter Indonesia as the private property of a foreigner who eventually stayed on to live there. This would be true of heirlooms such as the Han Dynasty hill-jar on page 109. Ceramic objects were also brought in by religious pilgrims (such as the pilgrim's bottle on page 110) and or by priests, like the Buddhist *kendi*, on page 98.

The roots of Southeast Asia

The *kendi* is an item found throughout history all over Southeast Asia. The origins of this bulbous flask form are not yet known, but clay *kendi* have been made in Indonesia since the prehistoric period (see pages 96-7). *Kendi* are known to have been used in Myanmar, Thailand, Cambodia, Vietnam, Malaysia, and the Philippines. Its function in Indonesia was—and in many places still is—as a ritual vessel for holy water as well as for everyday drinking water.

The Ceramics Collection of the National Museum in Jakarta provides much material evidence of the Indonesian archipelago's long history of international trade in the region, and it does so through objects of great beauty.

PLATE
This plate; made of porcelain, originally came from China (Ming Dynasty, *c.* 15th century), and was found in Jambi, Sumatra.
Size: 44 cm diam.; *Inv. No*: 147;
Gift of E.W. van Orsoy de Flines, 1959.

While large plates were not much used among the Chinese, beginning in the 13th century there were numerous orders from the Islamic kingdoms of Southeast Asia, to accommodate the Islamic custom of communal dining.

FUNERARY *KENDI* [OPPOSITE]

Material: Earthenware
Origin: Melolo, East Sumba (Neolithic)
Size: 32.8 cm high x 20.8 cm diam.
Inv. No: 4327
Acquired: 1939

This *kendi*, discovered during the
excavation of a Neolithic site in East
Sumba, has anthropomorphic
features, probably added as a tribute
to ancestral spirits in return for their
protection. *Kendi* decorated in this
manner are thought to have been
used for ritual and as burial goods.
They are usually found with other
objects buried in large urns with a
human skeleton. This type of
secondary burial would be
performed only for people of
high rank.

CEREMONIAL *KENDI* [RIGHT]

Material: Earthenware
Origin: Melolo, East Sumba
           (Neolithic)
Size: 25 cm high; 19 cm diam.
Inv. No: 1943
Acquired: 1923

This *kendi* was found together
with ten human skulls and bones in
a funerary urn *in situ* at a burial site
in a small village in Eastern Sumba.
Besides its especially pleasing
shape, what makes it unique is its
single opening, for both filling and
pouring, at the tip of the spout.
This, and the anthropomorphic
figure that forms the neck,
indicates that it was used in
religious rites as well as for
burial goods.

MAJAPAHIT HEAD

Material: Terracotta
Origin: Panataran, East Java
Date: 14th century
Size: 15 x 16 cm
Inv. No: 7149
Acquired: *c.*1940

This terracotta sculpture, with its
finely shaped features, wears a
hairstyle typical of terracotta
figures from the Majapahit era.

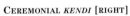

TANG WATER VESSEL (*KENDI*)

Material: Glazed earthenware
Origin: China, Tang Dynasty,
　　　　　c. 8th century AD
　　　　　Palembang, Sumatra
Size: 25.5 cm high
Inv. No: 3179f
Gift of E.W. van Orsoy de Flines,
1959

This *kendi* shows obvious formal influence from the Indian water vessel (*kundika*). Vessels of this type are seen in carved reliefs at Candi Borobudur, and are often called *kendi Buddha*. It is believed that they were once used as holy water vessels by Buddhist priests and novices visiting the kingdom of Sriwijaya in the 7th to 10th centuries. This object is very rare.

TANG JAR (*GUCI*)

Material: Polychrome glazed
            earthenware
Origin: China, Tang Dynasty,
            c. 8th century,
            Jambi, Sumatra
Size: 18 cm high
Inv. No: 3050f
Gift of E.W. van Orsoy de Flines, 1959

This jar was thrown on a wheel.
The lead-based polychrome glaze
was applied with a technique
similar to the resist technique in
batik-making: the areas to remain
white are covered with a layer of
wax. In China, this would have
been called a three-colour ceramic,
or *sancai*.

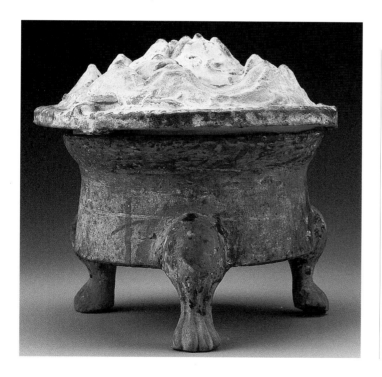

HILL-JAR

Material: Glazed earthenware
Origin: China, Han Dynasty
            c. 206 BC-220 AD,
            Jambi, Sumatra
Size: 19 cm high
Inv. No: 3159
Gift of E.W. van Orsoy de Flines, 1959

The high relief in the shape of a
several-peaked mountain *(boshan)*
symbolises the Taoist abode of the
gods, and is the source of the name
'hill-jar' given to these objects.
    Ceramics from the Han Dynasty
are generally made of fine red clay.
This example has an uneven green
lead glaze which, as a result of long
burial, has changed to a dull white
and has flaked off in some places.
It is thought that Han Dynasty
ceramics were brought to
Indonesia as heirlooms by
emigrating Chinese families. This
example might have been used as a
burial object, or it might have been
buried in a natural disaster.

SONG VASE [ABOVE]
Material: Glazed earthenware
Origin: China, Song Dynasty
  c. 12th–13th century,
  Majene, South Sulawesi
Size: 22 cm high
Inv. No: 2411
Gift of E.W. van Orsoy de Flines, 1959

The vase is decorated in high relief with flowers and leaves that have been appliquéd to the body and embellished with a technique called *sgraffito*; the brown slip has been incised to reveal the contrasting layer beneath. This vase is a Cizhou piece, of which many were made in northern China.

YUAN VASE [RIGHT]
Material: Porcelain
Origin: China, Yuan Dynasty
  c. 14th century,
  Bali
Size: 26.5 cm high
Inv. No: 3837
Gift of E.W. van Orsoy de Flines, 1959

The mouth of this vase was either chipped accidentally or broken intentionally to fasten the silver collar piece, decorated with a floral motif. The vase itself is not a particularly fine example of ceramic work, but the piece is rare because of the copper-red colour, which is extremely difficult to produce.

JAR (*GUCI*)
Material: Porcelain
Origin: China, Song Dynasty
  c. 11th–12th century
  Pasuruan, East Java
Size: 16 cm high
Inv. No: 1004
Gift of E.W. van Orsoy de Flines, 1959

This piece is one of the finest in the Museum's ceramics collection, and is expertly formed of fine, pure white porcelain. The 'carved' peonies motif, incised with 'comb markings', was applied with exquisite skill. This is also called a '*Quinbai* good'.

According to ceramics experts, the collection of Vietnamese ceramics at the National Museum is one of the largest in the world, and contains many rare and unusual pieces.

SIRIH LIME POT
Material: Glazed stoneware
Origin: Vietnam, *c.* 16th century
           Lampung, Sumatra
Size: 16.5 cm high
Inv. No: 3742
Gift of E.W. van Orsoy de Flines, 1959

The form of this small pot was inspired by the custom of chewing betelnut (*sirih*)—a practice widespread in Asia, and a traditional expression of hospitality. The green-glazed handle appears to be in the form of a rolled quid.

PLATE
Material: Porcelain
Origin: Vietnam
           c. 15th–16th century,
           Mandar, Sulawesi
Size: 36.5 cm diam.
Inv. No: 4093f
Gift of E.W. van Orsoy de Flines, 1959

The deep blue beneath the transparent glaze, and the artist's unusual style of painting, make this a piece of fine heirloom quality.

VASE [OPPOSITE]
Material: Glazed porcelain
Origin: Vietnam
           c. 15th century
           Ternate, Maluku (Moluccas)
Size: 26 cm high
Inv. No: 1759
Gift of E.W. van Orsoy de Flines, 1959

The body of this vase was painted beneath the glaze with a decoration of peonies and 'flaming pearls', in a rare blue-violet that is striking against the white ground of the porcelain.

Ternate was at one time a centre of spice production. The great profits produced by the spice trade allowed the purchase of high-quality imported ceramics such as this. It is in excellent condition, due to the fact that until recently ceramics and other valued objects were carefully stored in the ground to protect them from theft and the damage of war. They would be unearthed on special occasions.

BOTTLE

Material: Glazed porcelain
Origin: China, Ming Dynasty
c. 15th century,
Tobelo, Halmahera Island
Size: 25 cm high
Inv. No: 1706
Gift of E.W. van Orsoy de Flines, 1959

This bottle is unusual for the four globes painted on the body, emblazoned with the word 'ESPERO', meaning 'I hope'. They are the emblem of King Manuel of Portugal (1469-1521). The bottle seems to have originated during the 16th century when Portuguese traders held a monopoly in the spice region of Halmahera, North Moluccas. The globe emblem appears on another item in the Museum's collections: a monument named 'Padrao', found in the Old City of Jakarta, which solemnised an agreement between the Portuguese and the ruler of Jayakarta, Prince Wijayakrama, in 1527. This rare bottle, made to order by Portuguese traders as a show of patriotism, appears to have been made only in the province of Fujian.

PLATE

Material: Porcelain
Origin: China (unknown)
Found on Ternate, Maluku
Size: 35 cm diam.
Inv. No: 3602
Acquired: 1957

This plate depicts an expedition launched in search of the Isles of Fortune. It is thought to have been made in Kiangsi, in southeastern China.

PLATE
Material: Glazed and enamelled
            porcelain
Origin: China, Ming Dynasty
            c. 17th century
            Lampung, Sumatra
Size: 36.5 cm diam.
Inv. No: 1495
Gift of E.W. van Orsoy de Flines, 1959

This large Ming plate is painted
with an enamel overglaze known as
wu t' sai ('five colours'). The
Arabic calligraphy is expertly
executed.

This plate is classified as a
'Swatow good', denoting the
Chinese ceramic exports of the
16th and 17th centuries (after the
harbour city of Shantou,
Guangdong, from where they were
shipped).

JAR (*GUCI JANTAN*) [RIGHT]
Material: Stoneware
Origin: China, Ming Dynasty
            c. 17th century,
            Southwest Kalimantan
Size: 84.5 cm high
Inv. No. : 364
Acquired: 1931

This tall Ming jar is called a 'male
jar' (*guci jantan*). It is used as
bride price, among other ritual
purposes, and is highly prized as an
heirloom among the people of the
Kalimantan interior. This particular
jar was found in a longhouse in
southwestern Kalimantan.

VASE [OPPOSITE]
Material: Celadon glazed stoneware
Origin: China, Ming Dynasty
            c. 16th–17th century,
            Serang, West Java
Size: 34.75 cm high
Inv. No: 1645
Gift of E.W. van Orsoy de Flines, 1959

This tall, cylindrical vase is made
of rather thick stoneware.
Characteristically of Ming Dynasty
celadon, it is completely covered
with decoration. Incised
chrysanthemums adorn the body;
the shoulder and base show
geometric motifs; and the left and
right shoulder are appliquéd with
Taotiah, or giant's head, motifs.

This vase is considered of good
quality, and was found in Serang,
near Banten in the province of
West Java. From the 15th to the
19th centuries, Banten was the
seat of an Islamic kingdom on the
north coast, a centre of local and
international trade. It is classified
as a trade good.

GUCI [LEFT]
Material: Stoneware
Origin: Myanmar
        c. 14th–16th century
        Banten, West Java
Size: 25.5 cm high; diam. 24 cm
Inv. No: 1534
Gift of E.W. van Orsoy de Flines, 1959

Ceramic ware from Myanmar makes up a very small portion of the Museum's collection, and these have mostly been found in Sumatra (Aceh, Bengkulu, and Lampung) and in West Java (Banten). In Dutch historical records of the 17th century, Myanmar ceramics are mentioned as having been taken to Aceh and Banten. Whether this vase was used as burial goods, or merely as a household item, is not certain.

VASE [RIGHT]
Material: Glazed stoneware
Origin: Cambodia
        c. 10th–12th century,
        West Kalimantan
Size: 35.5 cm high
Inv. No: 5000
Gift of E.W. van Orsoy de Flines, 1959

This Khmer vase was probably made in the region of (present-day) northeastern Thailand between the 10th and 12th centuries. Ceramics workshops are thought to have begun producing in this area around 900 AD and to have stopped in the 14th century. Khmer ceramics are very rarely found in Indonesia.

ELEPHANT STATUE
Material: Stoneware
Origin: Thailand, Swankhalok
        c. 15th century
        Found at the head waters of
        the Pari River, Matalibo,
        South Kalimantan
Size: 50 cm high
Inv. No: 3655
Gift of E.W. van Orsoy de Flines, 1959

The statue depicts an elephant with two riders; shield-carrying attendants stand at each of the elephant's feet. The piece is made of extremely heavy grey stoneware, glazed in dark brown and cream white. On the elephant's back is a small bowl for use as a censer. Elephants have always been beloved among the people of Thailand because of their usefulness in everyday work and their part in Buddhist temple ceremonies.

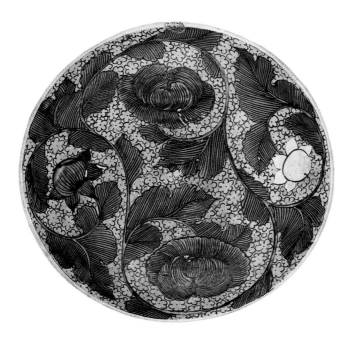

PLATE
Material: Glazed and enamelled
           porcelain
Origin: Japan, Arita
           c. 17th century,
           Banyuwangi, East Java
Size: 37 cm diam.
Inv. No: 800
Gift of E.W. van Orsoy de Flines, 1959

This plate is classified as Kutani
style, which although common in
Japan, is rarely found in Indonesia.

PILGRIM'S BOTTLE [RIGHT TOP]
Material: Unglazed earthenware
Origin: Middle East (Arabia?)
           c. 18th–19th centuries,
           Brebes, Central Java
Size: 37 cm high
Inv. No: 983
Gift of E.W. van Orsoy de Flines, 1959

A *dorak*, or pilgrim's bottle, which
would have been filled with holy
water on completion of the
pilgrimage to Mecca and taken
home and treasured as an
heirloom.

FLASK [RIGHT BOTTOM]
Material: Glazed stoneware
Origin: Rhineland, Germany
           c. 18th–19th century,
           Banten, West Java
Size: 25 cm high
Inv. No: 2780
Gift of E.W. van Orsoy de Flines, 1959

Many examples of flasks like this
one, which were used to hold
liquor, have been found in places
where the Dutch East Indies
Company had offices. Because of
their unique motif—the face of a
bearded man and a flower—these
bottles earned the name 'Pak
Jenggot' ('Mister Whiskers').

***KENDI* [OPPOSITE]**
Material: Glazed and enameled
           porcelain
Origin: Japan, Arita
           c. 17th–18th century,
           Banten, West Java
Size: 21.5 cm high
Inv. No: 4065
Gift of E.W. van Orsoy de Flines, 1959

The Chinese began exporting
kendi during the Tang Dynasty,
producing only to fill demand
abroad because there was none at
home. Eventually Japan, Vietnam,
and Thailand joined in the
production and exported to
Southeast Asia.

CHAPTER 5

BRONZE

O bjects in bronze have an innate nobility. More than any other metal, this copper alloy is at once durable and able to assume precise forms with very fine detail. Its permanence makes bronze objects a valuable record of human life. And it rings.

Evidence of the first uses of metal as a material for making objects has been found in the Middle East dating back to 10,500-8,500 years ago, and in Southeast Asia from around 3,000 BC, spreading from South China by way of Tonkin and Annam in what is now Vietnam. The Bronze Age culture known as Dongson (after the archeological site in Annam excavated in 1924), flourished in the 3rd or 4th century BC. Its bronze-casting techniques spread to Indonesia around 300 BC; and although the Dongson culture died out in the first century AD, its influence was felt in Indonesia for many centuries.

The metal objects found from Indonesia's Bronze-and-Iron Age include those of gold as well, but bronze is by far the most prevalent. This may be because of the region's rich natural supplies of copper and tin. (Bronze is generally composed of 90% copper and 10% tin and/or lead).

Indonesian bronze artefacts vary greatly in form, use, and iconography—a diversity that began to appear in the Bronze-and-Iron Age and reached its peak during the period of classical Javanese culture in the 14th century. These artefacts can be classed generally into two major categories: objects for everyday use; and sacred objects.

A picture of diversity

One of the most prevalent bronze objects found in the archipelago is the kettledrum. In 1902, the Austrian ethnologist F. Heger proposed a classification of bronze kettledrums into four types, based on their form, structure, size, decorative style and dissemination. The type classed as Heger Type I is the one most commonly found in Indonesia. (A fine example is presented on page 117.) These kettledrums seem to have originated in the Dongson culture, but there is evidence that they were produced in Java and Bali many centuries later.

The diversity of form and style of these bronze artefacts also reveals a variety of production techniques. Simple metal objects were generally made by forging (a process in which metal is heated and then formed by beating), while complex or unique objects were cast in moulds by either 'direct' or 'indirect' methods. Cast objects such as weapons sometimes underwent a secondary forging. Joins were made with rivets or by soldering.

Methods of casting

With direct casting, the heated metal is poured directly into a mould of clay or stone in which an impression of the desired shape has been carved. This produces a solid object with one flat side. Symmetrical objects may be cast in a two-piece (bi-valve) mould. Multi-moulds are formed of smaller (sub-)moulds connected to form one unit. Once cool, the object is removed and the mould may be re-used.

Indirect casting—also called 'lost wax' (*cire perdue*) casting—is far more complex. The desired form is first modelled in wax. A network of wax strips is added to the model, to provide passageways for the molten bronze to flow—and for air to escape—during the few seconds of casting. The wax object is then encased in a mould—a porridge of fireproof material (a mixture of plaster or mud with powdered firebrick). Once dry, the mould is fired in a kiln, leaving it hard enough to withstand the pouring of the molten bronze. During the firing the wax burns off leaving a cavity in the negative shape of the original form, into which the hot bronze is poured.

While this technique is useful for very small objects like coins or jewellery, statuary of any size must be hollow. In this case, the original form is carved or modelled in a convenient material; but the founder's problem then is to achieve a thin hollow reproduction of that form in wax. This is done by first making a split negative mould of the original form in plaster or fine mud, often in many pieces if the shape is complicated. Once the negative piece-mould has hardened, it is coated with the necessary thickness of wax and filled with a core of the ceramic mould material. From here on the process is the same: wax 'runners' and vents are applied to strategic parts of the form; the casting mould is built up over the filled wax and fired; the wax burns off leaving a complex hollow shape in the precise form of the sculpture; and the molten metal is poured.

A high degree of skill on the part of both sculptors and bronze founders had developed by the time of Java's Hindu-Buddhist culture, a period that began around the 7th or 8th century AD in Sumatra and Central Java, spread to East Java, then culminated at the end of the 15th century. Like stone sculpture of the same era, bronze statuary was religious in nature, providing a physical point of focus for devotional rites. The durability of bronze has preserved details of dress and ornamentation that identify the statues, especially those within the Indian canon, which specifies the attributes to be displayed by particular deities. The objects they carry are symbolic of their particular powers. A study of religious statuary provides clues about the development of different religious cultures in various regions of the archipelago.

CEREMONIAL AXE
Ceremonial axes from Bandung, West Java (top)
and Landu, North Roti (bottom). Both pieces
date from the Bronze Age and are 74 cm and 89
cm long respectively.
Inv. Nos: 1436 (top), 1441 (bottom)
Gift of the Resident of Bandung,1898 (top)
Gift of H. C. Humme, 1875 (bottom)

*Ceremonial axes of this sort were
generally used as burial goods.*

CEREMONIAL AXE

Origin: Ujung Pandang,
           South Sulawesi
Date: Bronze-and-Iron Age
Size: 70.5 x 45 x 8.3 cm
Inv. No: 1839
Acquired: 1933

This 'shoe-axe' is adorned with
Dongson-style motifs. The mask
image on the neck is thought to be
a general protective symbol against
malevolent forces.

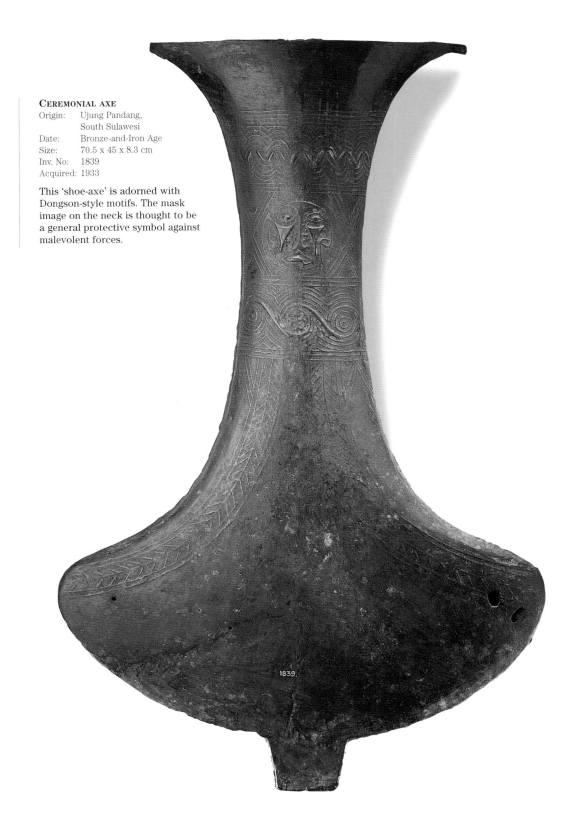

KETTLEDRUM (*NEKARA*)

Origin: Sangeang, Bima, Sumbawa
Date: Bronze-and-Iron Age
Size: 86.1 cm high; 111.5 cm diam.
Inv. No: 3367
Bequest of S. Kortleven, 1937

Like most of the kettledrums found in Indonesia, this is a Heger Type I, having a shoulder, body, and feet.

Nearly half the body of this drum is broken and lost, but the tympanum, extensively decorated with high relief patterns and four separately cast bronze frogs, is intact. The motifs on the tympanum include a 12-point star, stylised birds, flying cranes, and a variety of meanders, lines, and geometric patterns, typical of Dongson-style decoration. This drum was found in the burial grounds of a village on the island of Sangeang, and bequeathed by the former Dutch *Controleur*. At the time, the people of Sangeang worshipped this drum and had given it the name 'Saritasangsi'.

BRACELET [ABOVE]
Origin: Krui, Bengkulu, Sumatra
Date: Bronze-and-Iron Age
Size: 13 cm diam. x 3.1 x 3 cm
Inv. No: 5230
Acquired: 1941

The size and shape of this large,
heavy bracelet suggests that it was
worn on the leg or ankle.

BRACELET
Origin: Pasemah, Palembang,
           South Sumatra
Date: Bronze-and-Iron Age
Size: 7.5 cm diam.
Inv. No: 2184
Acquired: date unknown

This bronze bracelet is decorated
with a relief pattern around the
entire outer surface. The piece was
found at a burial site.

FIGURINE

Origin: Bangkinang, South Sumatra
Date: Bronze-and-Iron Age
Size: 9.5 cm high
Inv. No: 6000
Acquired: 1951

This dancing figure is thought to be a representation of ancestral spirits. It may have been worn as a pendant.

SPEARHEADS

Origin: Ciparay, Bandung, West Java
Date: Bronze-and-Iron Age
Size: Approx. 14 cm long
Inv. No: 423, 1424, 3040
Gift of Dr. P. V. van Stein Callenfels, 1937

Spearheads like these have been found throughout Java. Their symmetrical form indicates that they were cast in a bi-valve mould. The tips of the spearheads were strengthened by forging.

Three examples of Kuvera, the popular god of prosperity, traditionally portrayed with a protruding belly.

KUVERA [OPPOSITE]

Origin: Ngepoh, Badran,
Pemanggung, Central Java
Date: 8th-9th century
Size: 38 cm high
Inv. No: C.225 (8518)
Acquired: 1960

KUVERA [ABOVE LEFT]

Origin: Yogyakarta, Central Java
Date: 8th-9th century
Size: 15 cm high
Inv. No: 551b
Acquired: 1890

KUVERA

Origin: Surakarta, Central Java
Date: 8th-9th century
Size: 18 cm high
Inv. No: 547
Acquired: 1894

PADMAPANI [RIGHT]
Origin: Unknown
Date: 9th-10th century
Size: 7.5 cm
Inv. No: A.56/616
Acquired: 1974

An energetic representation of this Vajrayana Buddhist deity.

VAIROCANA AND CONSORT
Origin: Pati, Jepara, Central Java
Date: 12th-13th century
Size: 12 x 10 x 4.5 cm
Inv. No: 6021 (3570)
Acquired: 1892

Another Vajrayana piece. Vairocana's hands are in the *bhodyagrimudra* position; his consort's are held in the *dharmacakramudra* position.

HANGING BOWL

Origin: Bangil, East Java
Date: 12th-13th century
Size: 43 cm high, including chain
Inv. No: 3533
Acquired: date unknown

A hanging bronze pot for preserving the ashes of the dead. The lid is decorated with *repoussé* work in the form of a three-tiered mountain representing the mythical mountain Mahameru, believed to be the abode of the ancestors.

These three statues were found in 1931 when the government was laying water pipes in Palembang.

BRAHMA [NEAR RIGHT]
Origin: Boom Baru, Palembang, South Sumatra
Date: 11th-12th century
Size: 54.5 cm high
Inv. No: 6033
Acquired: 1931

This statue depicts the god Brahma with his characteristic four heads, astride his celestial mount, Hangsa.

DEITY [CENTRE]
Origin: Boom Baru, Palembang, South Sumatra
Date: 11th-12th century
Size: 46 cm high
Inv. No: 6034
Acquired: 1931

Depicted here is a god whose identity is not absolutely certain. The *prabhamandala* (halo) and his four arms attest to his divine status. He stands on the back of an animal that looks like a horned lion. From its resemblance to the image of the bull Nandi on the Gemuruh gold plaque (on page 135), it is presumed that this creature is Nandi and that the god he carries is therefore Shiva. The god's right hand holds a long, unidentified object; in his left rear hand is a lotus bud.

VISHNU
Origin: Palembang, South Sumatra
Date: 11th-12th century
Size: 57 cm high
Inv. No: 6032
Acquired: 1931

This statue depicts the god Vishnu standing atop his mount, Garuda.

LAMP

Origin: Juwana, East Java
Date: 1356
Size: 24 cm high
Inv. No: 1076
Acquired: 1892

A hanging oil lamp. The figure in meditation sits on the elevated floor of a 'floating' pavilion, attended by two female guardians who are pouring water into the surrounding pond. On the roof of the pavilion is an inscription in quadratic Kadiri script that gives the year as Saka 1278, or AD 1356.

WATERSPOUT

Origin: Cirebon, West Java
Date: 15th-16th century
Size: 41 cm high
Inv. No: 14313
Gift of Prince Adipati Muhamad
Djamal-Oed-Din, representative of the
Sultan Sepuh Cirebon, 1910

This bronze waterspout in the
form of a *naga* is from the ruins of
the water palace Sunyaragi,
belonging to the Kesepuhan palace
of Cirebon. In Javanese mythology,
the *naga* springs from the
underworld, which is always
connected with water.

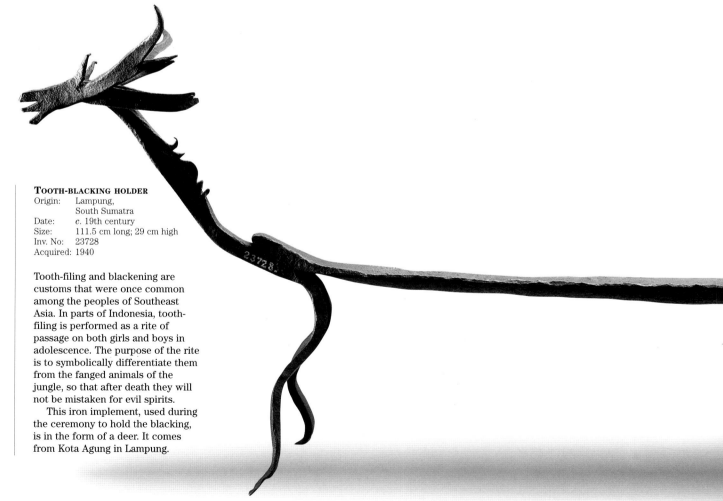

TOOTH-BLACKING HOLDER

Origin: Lampung,
            South Sumatra
Date: *c.* 19th century
Size: 111.5 cm long; 29 cm high
Inv. No: 23728
Acquired: 1940

Tooth-filing and blackening are
customs that were once common
among the peoples of Southeast
Asia. In parts of Indonesia, tooth-
filing is performed as a rite of
passage on both girls and boys in
adolescence. The purpose of the rite
is to symbolically differentiate them
from the fanged animals of the
jungle, so that after death they will
not be mistaken for evil spirits.
    This iron implement, used during
the ceremony to hold the blacking,
is in the form of a deer. It comes
from Kota Agung in Lampung.

WEIGHTS [FOUR PIECES]
Origin: Banjarmasin, Kalimantan
Date: *c.* 19th century
Size: From 2 to 9.5 cm high
Inv. Nos: 27342, 27343, 27350a, 27350b
Acquired: 1956

Representations of mythological
creatures from Indonesia's diverse
cultures are often seen in objects
like these bronze weights. They
depict a bird known as *kylin*,
which is associated with the upper
world of the gods. It has been
suggested that they symbolise
strength, courage, and fertility.
The weights are equal to 7.5g,
250g, and 750g.

PRECIOUS METALS

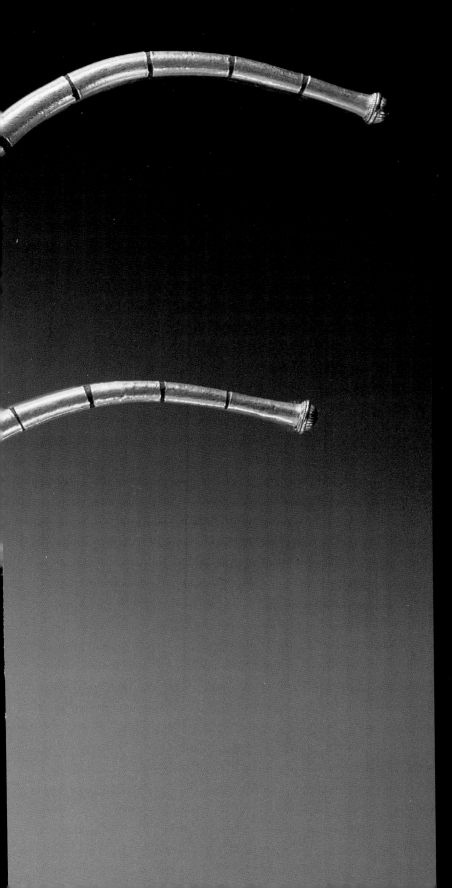

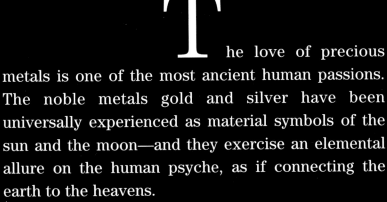

T he love of precious metals is one of the most ancient human passions. The noble metals gold and silver have been universally experienced as material symbols of the sun and the moon—and they exercise an elemental allure on the human psyche, as if connecting the earth to the heavens.

Geologically, gold and silver are the product of tectonic forces that twisted and buckled the earth's crust eons ago. The metals usually occur in granite quartz, which they penetrated in molten form far underground, forming seams of ore that catapulted upward under pressure from the surrounding subterranean materials. Some of the ore stayed underground and can be obtained only through mining. Those metals that burst to the surface either remained in the ore, showing as seams, or were carried away by erosion that left them in the ground as dust, flakes or nuggets—often swept by rivers, where they can be recovered by washing or dredging.

Indonesia has been well known as a source of gold and silver for millennia. Ancient Indians sought gold in 'the southern islands' (the Indonesian Archipelago); they called Sumatra 'Suvarnadwipa', the 'island of gold'. Tang Dynasty chronicles attest that Java produced a lot of gold and silver during the period 618-906 AD. The Canggal inscription, found at Gunung Wukir, Central Java and dated 732 AD, mentions that the Central Javanese kingdom was rich in gold mines.

Prehistoric objects of gold and silver have been found in many places in Indonesia, particularly in Java, Sumatra, Sulawesi, and Bali. These objects consist mainly of death masks and jewellery such as earrings and beads. Death masks were usually full face masks, put on the faces of the dead to guide the soul back to the proper body when it was called. Some of the masks were partial—mere strips of hammered gold indicating only the eyebrows, the nose and sometimes the mouth.

The Wonoboyo hoard

Objects made from precious metals found from Java's Classical Era (AD 5th-15th century) are in the form of statues of deities, as well as jewellery, regalia, and household utensils. In 1990, a remarkable hoard of gold and silver objects was found by farmers in a village near Wonoboyo, Central Java, about five kilometres from the Lara Jonggrang temple complex at Prambanan. The find, weighing around 35 kilograms in all, consists of household utensils, jewellery, ceremonial articles, and coins. They had been stored in four Tang Dynasty ceramic vessels and a bronze container and are thought to have been buried early in the 10th century AD. The 'Wonoboyo hoard', as it has become known, is the largest archeological find in Indonesia this century, and it is fortunate that its discoverers understood its historical and scientific importance.

Techniques

The techniques of metal-smithing (discussed in more detail in the previous chapter) are very old, and have changed little since prehistoric times. The most prevalent technique for making statuary, jewellery, and many implements is lost-wax casting. Another technique is to hammer the metal into a sheet and shape it by pressing or punching. Edges are joined by soldering or riveting. Decorative detail may be obtained by *repoussé* chasing to form a relief, or by incising the surface with a metal pen or tiny chisel.

These techniques are still widely practised in many parts of the Indonesian Archipelago. Precious metals play an important role in Indonesian societies—for instance, in identifying social rank, as in regalia or ceremonial ornaments restricted to certain groups. The *mamuli* on page 142 and the *lelancang* bowl on pages 144-45 are examples of this. Objects of gold also strengthen marriage alliances. The Indonesian term for bride-price is *emas kawin* ('wedding gold'). Like textiles and other ceremonial objects, precious metals are often integral to ritual.

In Indonesia, nearly every major ethnic group has its own smiths, held in high esteem by the community. In Java, the *keris*-maker is given the priestly honourific *mpu*—and with good reason: the *keris* is considered a weapon with supernatural powers. It is often decorated with precious metals in honour of both the owner and the spirit (*penunggu*) embodied within the *keris*. Although metalsmiths in Hindu India are not high in the caste order, the situation is different in the highlands of Hindu Bali. There the *pande* caste-clans, who specialise as iron smiths, gong smiths, and goldsmiths, are ranked as nobility—they are allowed nine roofs on their cremation towers, the same as kings—and in East Bali there is a village with numerous *Brahmana Buda* families that are goldsmiths. These skills flourished in Bali after the Majapahit conquest and subsequent migrations from the 12th-16th centuries. The *keris* on page 145, with its opulent handle and its sheath decorated with gold *repoussé*, is a good example of Balinese gold work in its Majapahit period.

Unusual treasures

The jewellery of East Nusa Tenggara is particularly beautiful, and it is associated with some unusual customary practices. In East Sumba, for instance, kings cultivated powerful slaves, who ate with their masters, advised them, and served as the king's double during certain ceremonies, decked out in royal gold.

As items of national treasure, the objects presented here have a value that is even greater than their very significant material worth: they are works of great artistry, and they bear an infinite wealth of meaning.

SCISSORS (*KACIP*)
A pair of 18th-19th-century scissors made of gold and iron, originating from Lombok.
Size: 20 x 8.5 cm; *Inv. Nos*: E.1020/18665d;
Acquired: 1986.

Kacip *are used for peeling and cutting areca nut,*
one of the ingredients of the betelnut quid.

BUDDHA [THIS PAGE]
Material: Gold
Origin: Desa Combre, Gunung Wilis,
            Kediri, East Java
Date: 10th century
Size: 9.5 cm high
Inv. No: LPPN 63/A.20
Acquired: 1963

An early Buddha, around his head is a ring of flames (*prabhavali*) with 11 points.

SHIVA [OPPOSITE, LOWER CENTRE]
Material: Silver
Origin: Pesindon, Kalialang, Ledok,
            Bagelen, Central Java
Date: 8th-9th century
Size: 8.6 cm high
Inv. No: 513/A. 45
Acquired: date unknown

A seated Shiva, carrying his attributes: trident (*trisula*), flask (*kendi*), fly whisk (*camara*), and rosary (*aksamala*). Behind the statue is a bronze halo (*prabhamandala*) surrounded by tongues of flame. A royal parasol (*chattra*) is fastened to the top. An unusual feature of this statue is the figure of the bull Nandi (Shiva's mount), facing out from the front of the statue's base.

SHIVA (SIWA MAHADEWA) [RIGHT]
Material: Silver
Origin: Central Dieng, Central Java
            (8th-9th century)
Size: 11.6 cm high
Inv. No: 6591/A.46
Acquired: date unknown

Shiva stands on a lotus blossom
pedestal holding his identifying
attributes. His *kain*, or hip cloth,
is covered by a tiger pelt; the head is
visible on his right thigh.

By the 9th century, Hinduism in
Java (alongside Buddhism) was
developing a distinctly Indonesian
character in which the Indian
pantheon was re-interpreted. Siwa
Mahadewa (or 'Shiva the Supreme
God') was the principal deity.

PADMAPANI [ABOVE]
Material: Silver
Origin: Unknown
Date: 8th-9th century
Size: 7.5 cm high
Inv. No: 616/A.56
Acquired: 1973

This mysterious little figure
sits on a wooden base that
is not original.

SHIVA [OPPOSITE]

Material: Gold
Origin: Gemuruh, Banyukembar,
  Leksono, Wonosobo, Central
  Java
Date: 9th century
Size: 20.5 x 10.8 cm x 1mm
Inv. No: A.24/517b
Acquired: 1903

Shiva is shown with his identifying
attributes, and also with the sun
and the moon, suggestive of the
dynamic 'positive-negative' nature
of the deity.

HARIHARA [LEFT]

Material: Gold *repoussé*
Origin: Gemuruh, Banyukembar,
  Leksono, Wonosobo, Central
  Java
Date: 9th century
Size: 36 cm high
Inv. No: A.30/517d
Acquired: 1903

A composite deity showing the
attributes of both Shiva and
Vishnu. Nandi and Garuda, their
respective mounts, crouch on
either side.

LINGAM

Material: Gold
Origin: Malang, East Java
Date: 10th-11th century
Size: 10.5 cm high
Inv. No: A.80/780
Acquired: 1780

Gold miniature of perhaps older
lingga-yoni forms that were used
as altars. The *lingga-yoni* is
symbolic of the dynamic
alternating quality of the universe
according to Shivite Hinduism.

RAMAYANA BOWL (CENTRE AND DETAIL BELOW)

Material: Gold
Origin: Wonoboyo, Central Java
Date: Early 10th century
Size: 28.8 x 14.4 x 9.3 cm
Inv. No: 8965
Acquired: 1991

One of the most opulent pieces in what is known as the 'Wonoboyo hoard', a cache of gold objects found by farmers in 1990 in the Central Javanese village of Wonoboyo. The bowl depicts scenes from the *Ramayana* epic in elaborate *repoussé* work.

COVERED BOWL

Material: Gold
Origin: Wonoboyo, Central Java
Date: Early 10th century
Size: 8.6 cm high; 10.1 cm diam.
Inv. No: 8930
Acquired: 1991

A finely modelled bowl with a
lotus leaf motif.

LADLE

Material: Gold
Origin: Wonoboyo, Central Java
Date: Early 10th century
Size: 14.5 cm long
Inv. No: 8992
Acquired: 1991

This 16-carat gold ladle was probably used for ritual ablutions, perhaps of consecrated statues. The handle was made separately and resembles that of a *keris*.

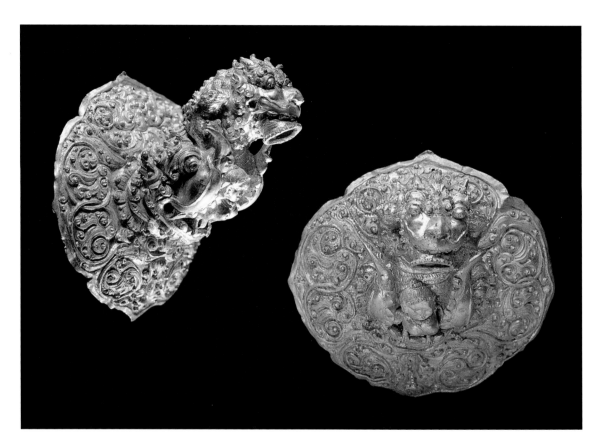

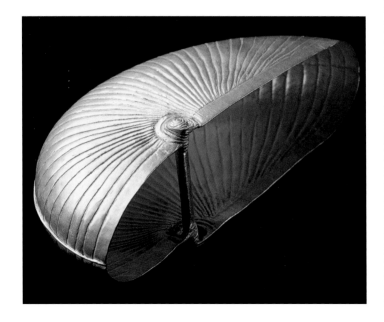

KENDI SPOUT [ABOVE]

Material: Gold
Origin: Wonoboyo, Central Java
Date: Early 10th century
Size: 5.7 cm high; 7.3 cm diam.
Inv. No: 8998
Acquired: 1991

This elaborate spout of a pouring vessel is in the form of a *makara* —a composite mythical beast with an elephant's trunk, a lion's mane, a parrot's beak and the tail of a fish. Images of *makara* often decorated temple gates in the 8th to 10th centuries.

WATER SCOOP

Material: Gold
Origin: Wonoboyo, Central Java
Date: Early 10th century
Size: 15.6 x 5.7 x 6.6 cm
Inv. No: 8997
Acquired: 1991

With luxurious whimsy, this gold water scoop mimics the shape of a banana-leaf water scoop.

PENDANT
Material: Gold
Origin: Wonosobo, Central Java
Date: Early 10th century
Size: 13.3 cm long
Inv. No: A.90/1546d
Acquired: Date unknown

This pendant would have held
magically protective ingredients.

LADLE HANDLE
Material: Gold
Origin: Wonoboyo, Central Java
Date: Early 10th century
Size: 6 cm long
Inv. No: 8991
Acquired: 1991

A separately cast piece made to fit
an object similar to the ladle on the
previous page.

PURSE

Material: Gold
Origin: Wonoboyo, Central Java
Date: Early 10th century
Size: 9.2 x 10 x 2.3 cm
Inv. No: 8916
Acquired: 1991

This gold purse is similar in form
to carrying cases still found in
Lombok and Tibet that are made of
humbler materials like rattan.

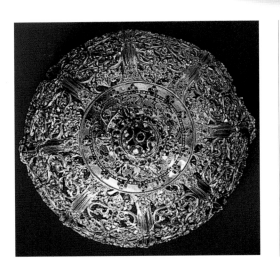

BANTEN CROWN [ABOVE AND BELOW LEFT]

Material:	Gold and precious stones
Origin:	Banten, West Java
Date:	16th century
Size:	17 cm high; 20 cm diam.
Inv. No:	E. 619
Acquired:	Date unknown

This crown was worn by the kings of Banten, from Sultan Maulana Hasanuddin in 1552 through to the reign of Sultan Muhammad Rafiudin in 1820.

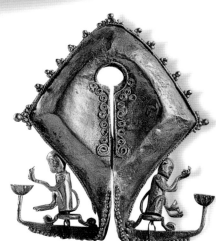

Hat (*Topi Toraja*) [RIGHT AND BELOW]

Material: Gold
Origin: Toraja, Sulawesi
Date: Early 19th century
Size: 13.5 cm high; 16 cm diam.
Inv. No: E.1350
Acquired: 1997

This gold hat, worn by the nobility, is ornamented with *repoussé* figures and geometric designs. The buffalo motif reflects the important role of that animal in the daily life and the cosmology of the Toraja people.

Ornament (*Mamuli*) [OPPOSITE, BELOW RIGHT]

Material: Gold
Origin: Sumba
Date: 17th-18th century
Size: 10.2 cm high
Inv. No: E. 1199
Acquired: 1900

Mamuli are owned only by the nobility. They are part of a king's regalia—used as ritual objects, burial goods, and bride-price. They may be plain or heavily ornamented; decorative motifs include human figures, animals, and the 'tree of life' (*adung*) found also on Sumba's famed *ikat* cloth. *Mamuli* with human figures are considered very sacred; those with the *adung* motif could be used only by members of the king's family. In West Sumba, *mamuli* are worn as earrings; in East Sumba, as a necklace pendant. In the Lauli region of West Sumba, a pair of male and female *mamuli* is given by the groom's family to the bride's as bride-price. Heavily ornamented *mamuli*, which generally do not contain figures, are kept as altar pieces. In West Sumba, *mamuli* are worn by both men and women during ceremonies; they are also worn by female dancers in the Lauli and Anak Alang regions.

CEREMONIAL BOWL (*LELANCANG*) [OPPOSITE]

Material: Gold
Origin: Bali
Date: 14th-15th century
Size: 21 cm high, 44 cm diam.
Inv. No: E.749
Acquired: 1898

An elliptical golden basin on a carved wooden base, decorated with *repoussé* work; around the lip is a border of spirals and tendrils.

In Bali, where Hindu rites are still practised, the *lelancang* hold offerings for the deities, composed of fruit, flowers, betelnut, and ornaments of cut palm leaf. Until recently, *lelancang* of this sort could be used only by members of the aristocracy.

This piece was most likely to have been made by royal artisans; it is presumed to have come from Klungkung, made sometime during the 14th or 15th centuries.

KERIS [LEFT AND ABOVE]

Material: Gold, iron,
          precious stones, wood
Origin: Bali
Date: Late 18th century
Size: 68.5 cm long
Inv. No: E.795
Acquired: 1910

This Balinese *keris* has a characteristically ornate handle—a gold *raksasa* demon studded with precious stones. The sheath is made of fine wood with gold *repoussé* ornamentation. The profusion of golden objects at the 16th century court of Klungkung astonished the first Dutch visitors, and fanned the desire for the wealth of 'the Orient'.

CHAPTER 7

HISTORY

Historical relics—objects that are especially treasured for their link to the past—may be revered for a variety of reasons: for their intimate association with heroes; because they constituted treasure in their own time; or because time has rendered them significant.

Maps give a very particular view of the world, at once abstract and practical. As historical documents, they can reveal much—not only about places but also about the concerns and ideas of the map-maker. Navigational maps were of course instrumental in opening Indonesia to the world as European nations competed for the lucrative spice trade.

Coins record a network of material agreements. 'Numismatics', the term for the study of coins, finds its root in the Greek word meaning 'to distribute'; and although the coins most highly valued by collectors are the rare ones, it is the standardisation of coins that makes them useful and gives them, literally, their currency. The National Museum's Numismatics Collection alone can be read as a series of footnotes to the story that is Indonesia's history.

The objects presented here—historical relics, maps, coins, and paintings—illuminate fragments of that story, which begins with the advent of writing around the 5th century AD.

During the 5th century, traders from India and China began visiting settlements in the Indonesian Archipelago, which lay directly along their sailing routes. The spreading influence of Indian culture, and the flowering of the Hindu and Buddhist religions from the 5th through to the 15th century, gave rise to Hindu-Buddhist kingdoms, among them Tarumanagara, Sriwijaya, Mataram, Kadiri, Singasari, and Majapahit.

The monetary system of these kingdoms was very like that of India. Of the various coins in circulation then, the most frequently found in Indonesia is the *mâsa* from the 10th-century Central Javanese kingdom of Mataram. These were produced by the 'hot blank' technique, when the metal is still soft; the resulting quality is crude. The later 'cold blank' technique required more force and gave a crisper result .

The rise of Islam

While Majapahit crumbled at the turn of the 16th century, powerful Islamic-influenced trading kingdoms began to emerge around the archipelago, among them Aceh, Demak, Banten, Cirebon, Mataram, Palembang, Banjarmasin, Jambi, and Sumbawa. Coins of the Islamic kingdoms were inscribed with the sultan's name and the year, according to the Islamic calendar, in Arabic or Arab-Malay script. It was around this time that Europeans began to arrive in Indonesia in pursuit of the spice trade.

The first Europeans to arrive were the Portuguese, who after conquering Malacca in 1511, proceeded further east to the 'Spice Islands' in the Moluccas. At almost the same moment, the Spanish arrived from the Pacific. The Portuguese established an outpost on Ternate in 1522; the Spanish set up on the nearby rival island of Tidore. The military superiority of the Europeans at this time lay in their gun and ship-building technology—in the ability to carry heavy guns, such as the bronze cannon on the facing page. Other European nations soon followed. For most of the 17th century, the English were allowed to operate from the West Javanese kingdom of Banten. But it was Holland that eventually became predominant.

The arrival of the Dutch

The Dutch first arrived in Indonesia in 1596 under the leadership of Cornelius de Houtman; in 1602, they established a trading company, the *Vereenigde Oost Indische Compagnie* (VOC). The VOC's policy of commercial monopoly led it to exert territorial control as well, which brought it into conflict with the kingdoms of Mataram, Banten, Aceh, Banjarmasin, Palembang, and Pontianak, among others. The treaties on page 164 remind one that the VOC tried to use diplomacy in pursuit of its interests; but Dutch rule was more often won by force. The punishment of rebelling factions in the Moluccas is recorded in the *The Capture of Loki, Ceram* (page 165). Indonesia felt the effect of the Napoleonic wars in Europe when France occupied the Netherlands and Indonesia became a French territory (1806-1810). It then became a British colony under Sir Stamford Raffles from 1811 to 1816. When Holland regained her colonies under the Vienna Congress of 1815, the Indonesian territories—now expanded after British annexations—came under the government of the Netherlands East Indies.

This caused considerable opposition among the kingdoms in Palembang, Sulawesi, Aceh, Jambi, and West Sumatra. Wars of resistance between 1825 and 1830, led in Java by Prince Diponegoro, caused heavy losses on both sides, but ultimately failed due to difficulties in consolidation among the Indonesians. Nonetheless, the rebellion prefigured the successful anti-colonial movement of the mid-20th century, and Diponegoro is revered today as the first revolutionary of the Indonesian nation. The Dutch colonial government lasted until 1942 when it left the archipelago to the invading Japanese, an occupation that ended with the Allied victory in August 1945 and the declaration of a free Indonesia.

The twentieth century

The determination of Indonesians to participate on an equal footing with Western nations may be seen in the rise of European-style painting among Indonesian artists. In the mid-20th century, easel painting was arguably the most prestigious form of European art, and thus an attractive medium for Indonesian artists who wanted to establish their place in the international community. Other Indonesian artists, such as the Balinese painters formed by the Pita Maha artists' group of the 1930s, found that contact with the West brought a heightened sense of their ethnic identity. This dynamic between modern and traditional, between unity and diversity, is intrinsic to the character of Indonesia today.

JAVANESE CEREMONIAL CANNON
This 18th century bronze cannon from Mangkunegoro,
Solo, is 54 cm long and has a diameter of 8 cm and a
bore of 2 cm.
Inv. No: 199; *Acquired*: 1983.

*Commemorates the coronation in 1727 of
Pakubuwono II, King of Mataram.*

BELL ('KYAI LINDU')
Material: Bronze
Size: 79 cm high; 48 cm diam.
Origin: Bangkalan, Madura
Date: 19th century
Inv. No: 19/9487
Acquired: 1900

The bell is inscribed in Old
Javanese script saying that it was
commissioned by Cakra-Adiningrat
II of Madura in 1742.

PORTUGUESE SHIP'S CANNON
Material: Bronze
Size: 82 cm long, 14 cm diam.,
            3.6 bore
Origin: Portugal
Date: 16th-17th century
Inv. No: 59/22767
Acquired: Date unknown

The Portuguese origin of this
cannon is evident from the insignia
on the base, in the form of a shield
and crucifix. Insignia like this were
seen on Portuguese coins
circulating at the time both in
Portugal and in its colonies,
including eastern Timor.

DIPONEGORO'S SADDLE

Material:	Cloth, leather, iron
Size:	Saddle: 80 cm long;
	68 cm wide
	Stirrups: 13 x 12 cm
Origin:	Yogyakarta, Central Java
Date:	19th century
Inv. No:	271
Acquired:	1978

Diponegoro (1785-1855), the eldsest son of Sultan Hamengku-buwono III, was born into an era of convulsion and decline in Central Java. He was raised by his royal grandmother in the countryside, where he studied Javanese classics and Islamic religious texts. Meanwhile, the kingdom was afflicted by court intrigue, European interference, popular discontent, and natural disasters. In his early twenties the prince underwent a series of mystical experiences in which he was called upon to become king of Java.

Another 20 years of turbulence passed before he judged the situation ripe for action and led the Javanese elite in a revolt against the Dutch in the Java War (1825-1830). The rebellion failed, but it prefigured the movement for independence that was finally successful in the mid-20th century.

DIPONEGORO'S SPEAR

Material:	Wood, metal wire, iron,
	gemstones, gold
Size:	98 cm long, 3.2 cm diam.
Origin:	Yogyakarta, Central Java
Date:	19th century
Inv. No:	270
Acquired:	1978

The three-faceted spearhead is engraved with a leaf tendril motif; the collar joining the shaft and the blade is gold-encrusted and set with precious stones to form the shape of a heart. The body of the shaft is wrapped with wire.

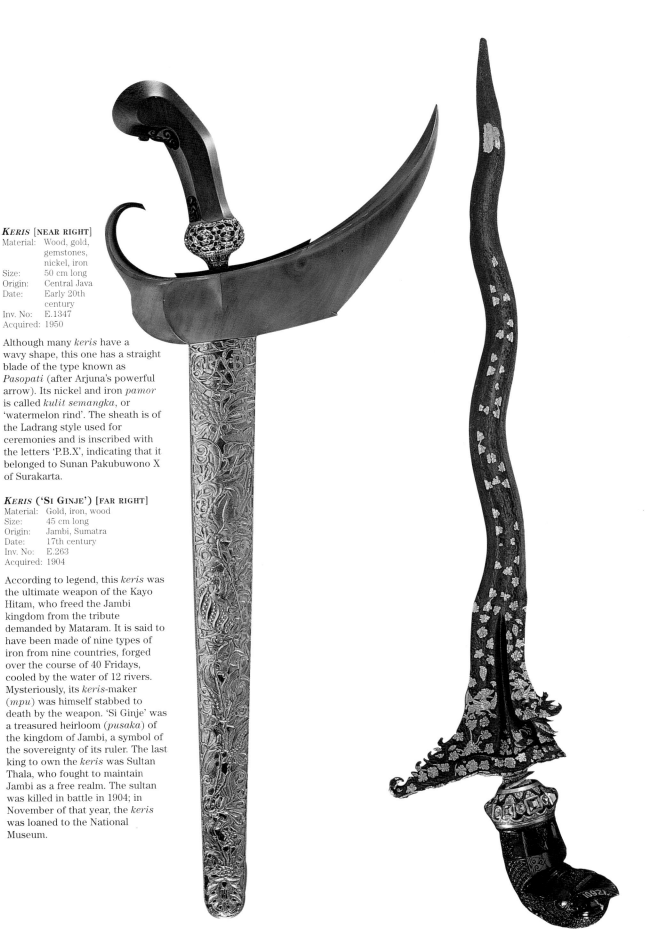

KERIS [NEAR RIGHT]

Material:	Wood, gold, gemstones, nickel, iron
Size:	50 cm long
Origin:	Central Java
Date:	Early 20th century
Inv. No:	E.1347
Acquired:	1950

Although many *keris* have a wavy shape, this one has a straight blade of the type known as *Pasopati* (after Arjuna's powerful arrow). Its nickel and iron *pamor* is called *kulit semangka*, or 'watermelon rind'. The sheath is of the Ladrang style used for ceremonies and is inscribed with the letters 'P.B.X', indicating that it belonged to Sunan Pakubuwono X of Surakarta.

KERIS ('SI GINJE') [FAR RIGHT]

Material:	Gold, iron, wood
Size:	45 cm long
Origin:	Jambi, Sumatra
Date:	17th century
Inv. No:	E.263
Acquired:	1904

According to legend, this *keris* was the ultimate weapon of the Kayo Hitam, who freed the Jambi kingdom from the tribute demanded by Mataram. It is said to have been made of nine types of iron from nine countries, forged over the course of 40 Fridays, cooled by the water of 12 rivers. Mysteriously, its *keris*-maker (*mpu*) was himself stabbed to death by the weapon. 'Si Ginje' was a treasured heirloom (*pusaka*) of the kingdom of Jambi, a symbol of the sovereignty of its ruler. The last king to own the *keris* was Sultan Thala, who fought to maintain Jambi as a free realm. The sultan was killed in battle in 1904; in November of that year, the *keris* was loaned to the National Museum.

GOBOG COIN [UPPER LEFT]
Material: Brass
Size: 45.8 mm diam./41 gms
Origin: Majapahit (Hindu Java)
Date: 14th century
Inv. No: None
Acquired: Date unknown

Gobog coins were generally large, measuring between 35 and 75 mm in diameter. Their size and near-perfect roundness suggest that they were cast. Earthenware moulds for *gobog* have been found in and around Trowulan, where the Majapahit kingdom flourished during the 14th century.

MA COIN [CENTRE]
Material: Gold
Size: 8.18 mm diam./2.4 gms
Origin: Mataram (Hindu Java)
Date: 10th century
Inv. No: 2090/2759
Acquired: Date unknown

Conical in shape with an oval face, this coin has the Old Javanese character '*ma*', an abbreviation for *mâsa*, hand-struck on to the coin face.

MA COIN [BOTTOM]
Material: Gold
Size: 22.1 mm diam./18 gms
Origin: Mataram (Hindu Java)
Date: 10th century
Inv. No: 12982
Acquired: Date unknown

Imprinted on one face is the Old Javanese character '*ma*', within a rectangle. This coin, found in Tegal, Central Java, is an example of hammered coinage using the 'hot blank' technique.

RUPYAH/GULDEN [UPPER RIGHT]
Material: Silver
Size: 19.42 mm diam./3.17 gms
Origin: Utrecht, Holland
Date: 1857
Inv. No: 14629
Acquired: Date unknown

One side of this 1/4 gulden coin is inscribed in Malay-Arabic script, the other in Dutch with the insignia of the Dutch crown. This is an example of machinery-struck, or milled, coinage made with a die such as the one shown opposite, upper left.

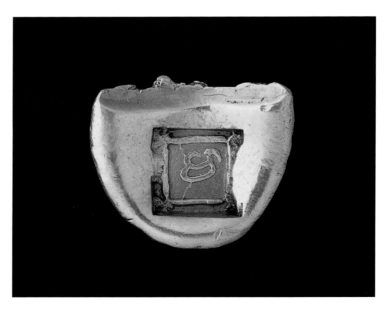

KASHA COIN
Material: Lead
Size: 20.81 mm diam./3.5 gms
Origin: Aceh, Sumatra
Date: 1851 (1267 Hijrah)
Inv. No: 2270/3140
Acquired: Date unknown

The Malay-Arabic script reads
'Bandar Darassalem Aceh'.

KETENG COIN
Material: Lead
Size: 18.8 mm diam./1.64 gms
Origin: Surakarta, Central Java
Date: 19th century
Inv. No: 2833/2971
Acquired: Date unknown

Cast in a mould similar to the one
below, lower right.

BATAVIA'S GENOOTSCHAP MEDAL
Material: Gold-plated silver
Size: 50 mm diam./57 gms
Origin: Holland
Date: c. 1778
Inv. No: 13749
Acquired: 1778

Commemorating the founding of
the Batavia Society.

COIN-CASTING MOULD
Material: Teakwood
Size: 45.6 x 6.2 cm
Origin: Surakarta, Central Java
Date: 19th century
Inv. No. : 13733
Acquired: Date unknown

For casting lead.

MACHINE-STRUCK COIN DIE [UPPER LEFT]
Material: Steel
Size: Upper die: 55.84 x 40 mm diam.
           Lower die: 40 x 32.4 mm diam.
Origin: Utrecht, Holland
Date: 1790
Inv. No: 13738a-b
Acquired: Date unknown

For minting *gulden* for the VOC.

COIN-CASTING MOULD [UPPER RIGHT]
Material: Stone
Size: 80 mm x 43.78 mm
Origin: Aceh, Sumatra
Date: 19th century
Inv. No: Not catalogued
Acquired: Date unknown

The *kasha* coin above left is an
example of the type of coin
produced by this bi-valve mould.

HAND-STRUCK COIN DIE [LOWER LEFT]
Material: Iron
Size: 77.42 x 19.28 mm
           62.26 x 13.36 mm
Origin: Madras, India
Date: 18th century
Inv. No: 13734, 13735
Acquired: Date unknown

For producing coins using the
coldblank technique.

l'Île de
BORNEO,
Suivant les memoires
des plus Celebres Navigateurs.
A LEIDE,
Chez PIERRE VANDER AA.

Linea Æqunocta lis.

Duytsche mylen 15 in een graed.

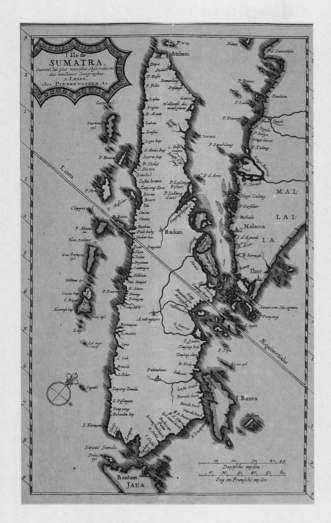

BORNEO (KALIMANTAN)
Material: Paper
Size: 18.5 x 15.5 cm
Origin: Leiden
Period: 17th century
Inv. No: 06
Acquired: Date unknown

A colour map made by Pierre van der A. A. of the island of Borneo in the 16th century. The shape of the island is not yet perfect. The equator is shown cutting through the centre of the island. Along the coast, cities and important kingdoms are drawn in: Benjarmasin (Banjarmasin), Succadana (Sukadana), and Sambas. The interior is shown as a mountainous region of jungle.

SUMATRA
Material: Paper
Size: 26.5 x 16 cm
Origin: Leiden
Period: 17th century
Inv. No: 07
Acquired: Date unknown

The map is simplified, and it is tilted to place the island vertically, with the equator shown on a diagonal.

Aceh became a great military and economic power under Sultan Iskandar Muda (r. 1607-36). He set high prices on the kingdom's gold and pepper, saying, 'Whoever wants to buy pepper must eat it from my hand.'

MOLUQUES (MALUKU)
Material: Paper
Size: 45 x 35 cm
Origin: Leiden
Period; 17th century
Inv. No: 292
Acquired: Date unknown

A colour map of a portion of the Moluccan Archipelago. The shape of the islands is inaccurate.

The Moluccas were the 'Spice Islands' so desired by Europeans, who sought the cloves and nutmeg that grew there. In the 17th century, Portugal, England, and Holland competed in the archipelago with local traders.

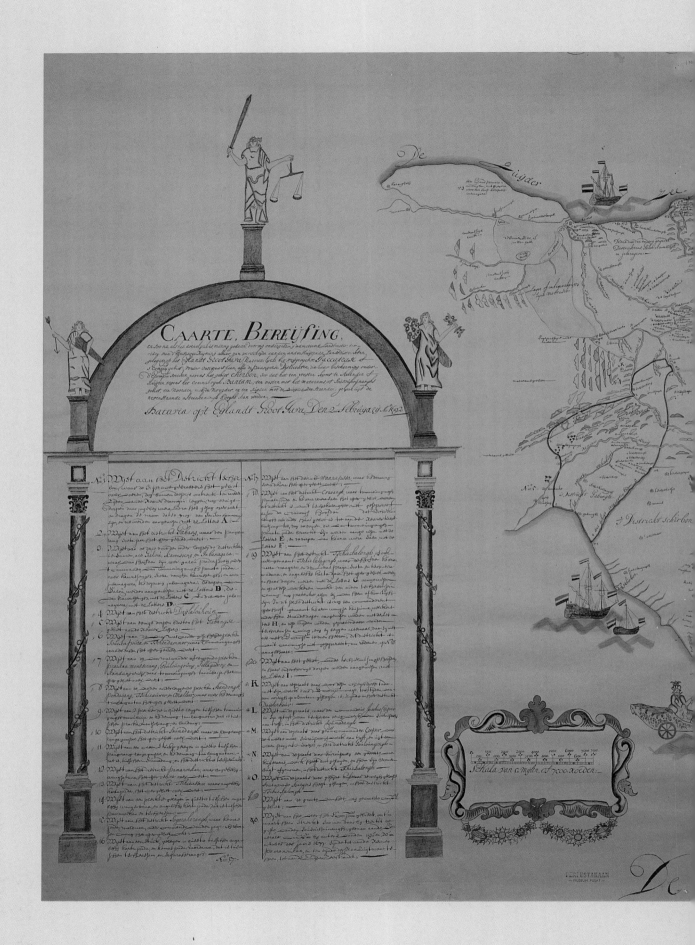

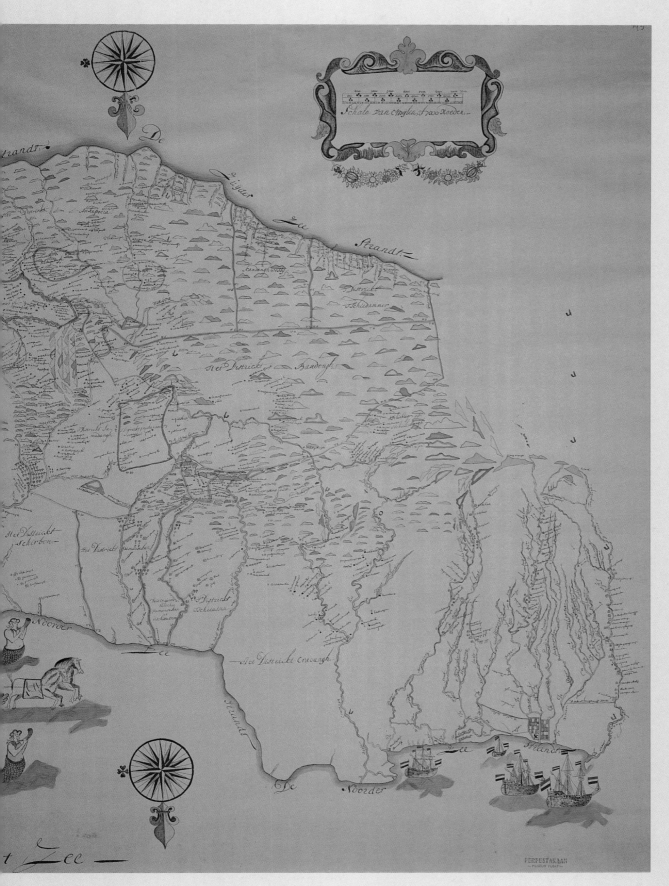

EYLANDT GROOT JAVA
(**THE GREAT ISLAND OF JAVA**)

Material: Paper
Size: 73 x 95 cm (2 sheets)
Origin: Batavia
Date: 1692
Inv. No: 11
Acquired: Date unknown

This hand-drawn map, dated
February 2nd 1692, was made by
the Land Affairs Office of the VOC
in Batavia. The land masses are
greatly simplified and do not
follow cartographic conventions:
north faces toward the bottom of
the map, as Dutch expeditions
would have seen it on their
approach from the sea.

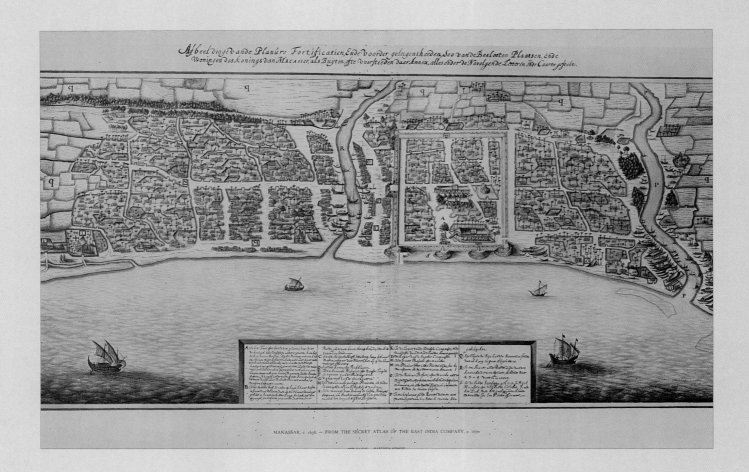

Afbeeldinge vande Planure Fortificatien, Ende Voorder gelegentheeden, Soo van de Beslooten Plaatsen, Ende Woningen des Konings van Macasser, als Bugten, ofte Voorsteeden daer Annex, alles onder de Navolgende Letteren Inde Caarte gesselt.

MAKASSAR, c. 1638. — FROM THE SECRET ATLAS OF THE EAST INDIA COMPANY, c. 1670

THE INDONESIAN ARCHIPELAGO
[LEFT]
Material: Paper
Size: 51 x 33 cm
Origin: Leiden
Period: Late 17th century
Inv. No: 275
Acquired: Date unknown

A navigational map of the Indonesian Archipelago and its surroundings at the end of the 17th century, made by Cornelius Daedts. It shows a portion of the archipelago in simplified form, as well as India, Siam (modern-day Thailand), China, Japan, Korea and the Philippines.

Such was 'the Orient' for 17th century Europeans.

MAKASAR
Material: Paper
Size: 102 x 50 cm
Origin: Leiden
Period: 1670
Inv. No: 258
Acquired: Date unknown

Makasar was the capital of the twin Gowa-Tallo kingdom, more usually called the Makasar kingdom. Gowa-Tallo had few natural resources to trade besides great quantities of rice. But the location was highly strategic. The town of Makasar, locally called Ujungpandang, was an important provisioning harbour for eastbound traders, and it became important as a place to buy Moluccan spices.

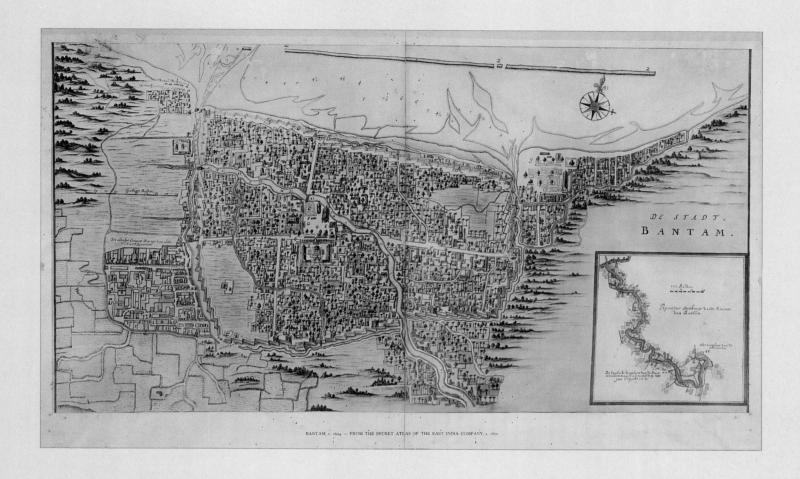

BANTAM, c. 1644 — FROM THE SECRET ATLAS OF THE EAST INDIA COMPANY, c. 1670

BANTAM (BANTEN, WEST JAVA)
Material: Paper
Size: 105 x 67.5 cm
Origin: Leiden
Period: 1670
Inv. No: 256
Acquired: Date unknown

This map of the coastal region near Old Banten (Banten Lama) from the year 1624 was based on a secret map belonging to the VOC. In 1526, Banten was subjugated by the religious sage Sunan Gunungjati and Molana

Hasanuddin of the Islamic kingdom of Demak, who later moved the capital from Banten Girang to Kota Surosowan. Molana Hasanuddin became the first sultan of Banten (r. 1552-1570), followed by his son Molana Yusup (r. 1570-1580), and Molana Muhammad from 1580 to 1596, in which year an important historical event took place—the arrival in Banten of the first Dutch in Indonesia, a trading expedition led by Cornelius de Houtman.

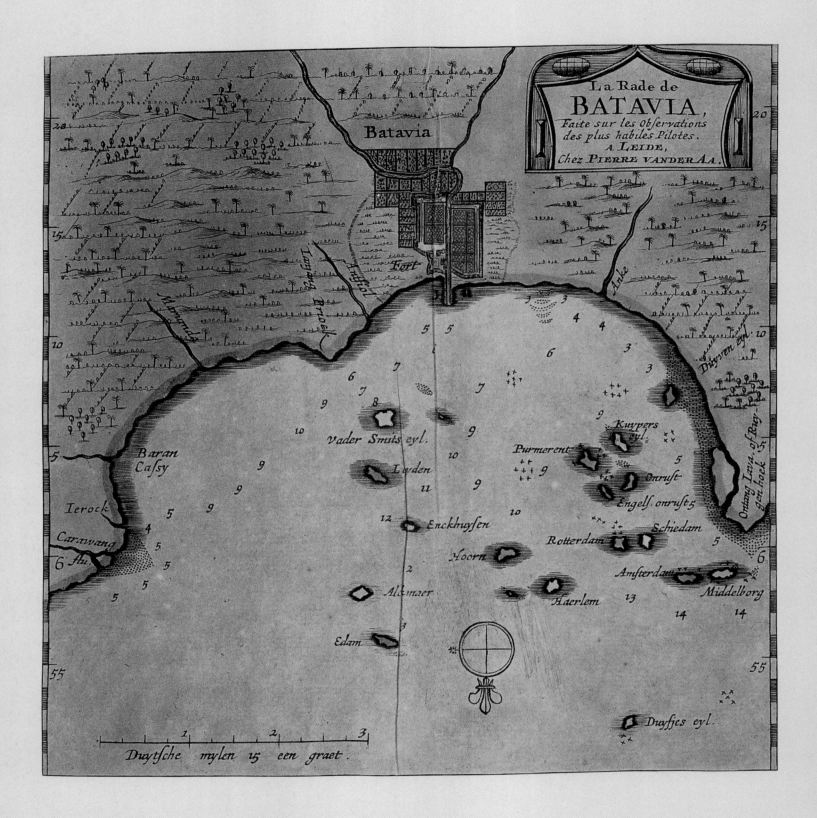

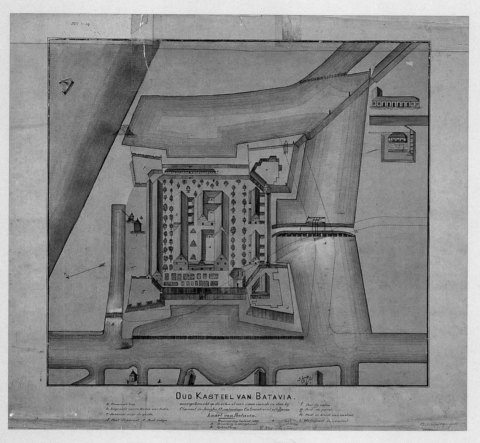

BATAVIA

Material: Paper
Size: 14 x 14 cm
Origin: Leiden
Period: 17th century
Inv. No: 02
Acquired: Date unknown

In 1611, the Dutch established an outpost in Jayakarta (as it was known then); VOC headquarters were far to the east in Ambon. But competition with the British (who were established in Banten) led the Dutch to move their seat to western Java.

In 1619 they attacked Jayakarta, burning everything but their fortress, and renamed the place Batavia. This printed colour map by Pierre Vander A. A., shows Batavia's harbour in the 17th century, with north to the bottom, as it would have appeared to mariners. It depicts the coast in the vicinity of the Ciliwung River delta, where Batavia stands surrounded by walls and canals.

During this period, life in Batavia became increasingly prosperous and secure, and the trend began for residents to move out of the city. The Governor-General, high officials of the VOC, and wealthy city residents bought estates on which they built handsome Dutch-style houses.

OUD KASTEEL VAN BATAVIA (OLD CASTLE OF BATAVIA)

Material: Paper
Size: 72 x 62 cm
Origin: Batavia
Period: 1883
Inv. No: 14
Acquired: Date unknown

A ground plan describing the fortress in Batavia between the years 1650 and 1883. This unusual map was originally made, in colour, in 1650 by Clement de Jongke and then re-made in May 1883. It shows the VOC offices and residences for VOC staff and troops. Each corner of the fortress had a name—Diamont, Ruor, Sapphiere, Pearl.

TREATY [UPPER LEFT]

Material: Paper
Size: 22.5 x 35 cm; 70 pages
Origin: Sulawesi
Period: September 1800
Inv. No: E.1337/18665 C
Acquired: Date unknown

An agreement between the Governor of Sulawesi and Andi Manatang of Rappang in the area controlled by Soemanga Roekka. The documents were signed by both parties and certified by sealing wax without a stamp. The text is in Malay script and Dutch, and includes a contract made by Albert George Brugman, Secretary of the *Inlandsch Zaken*, in the name of the Dutch Indies Governor-General, with Soemang Roekka of Rappang; the contract contains 20 articles. A sub-contract is appended, signed and sealed by Aroe Rappang and the Dutch.

TREATY [LOWER LEFT]

Material: Paper
Size: 22 x 34 cm; 82 pages
Origin: Kalimantan
Period: 18 April 1903
Inv. No: E.1338/18666
Acquired: Date unknown

A contract between the Prince of Pasir, Ibrahim Chalil Oedin, and Alexander Kroesen, Resident of South and East Kalimantan. The agreement comprises 34 articles each of which contains a number of sub-articles, written in Dutch and Arabic. It was made in September 1902 and signed on April 18th 1903, and bears the Islamic date, 20 Dzoelhijah 1320. Only one of the two parties signed the agreement—Sultan Pasir Ibrahim Chalil Oedin, along with his witnesses Prince Koesoemo Jayaningrat, Prince Mantrie and Prince Dipati.

THE CAPTURE OF LOKI, CERAM

Material: Paper
Size: 41.5 x 66.5 cm
Origin: Leiden
Period: 1670
Inv. No: 260
Acquired: Date unknown

Depicts the battle scene at Loki on June 27, 1652, based on a secret map belonging to the VOC.

During the 1630s and '40s, resistance to the VOC among the Moluccans threatened Dutch hegemony over the clove trade. In 1650 a palace coup deposed the unpopular sultan of Ternate. He was soon restored by the VOC; but the rebels regrouped on the island of Hoamoal and led a ferocious attack on Dutch settlements. The VOC retaliated in a series of brutal military campaigns, burning the clove plantations on Hoamoal and deporting the population.

Portrait of a Dutch Governor-General

Artist: Saleh Syarief Bustaman,
             born in Terboyo, Semarang,
             Central Java, 1807; d. 1880
Material: Oil on canvas
Size: 122.5 x 89.5cm
Period: 1867
Inv. No: 206
Gift of the artist, 1867

Raden Saleh, a widely travelled Javanese aristocrat, is considered to be one of the pioneers of modern Indonesian painting.

This painting is listed as a portrait of Johannes van den Bosch, Governor-General (1830-1833) and initiator of the notorious *cultuurstelsel*, 'forced cultivation',

system in Java. Because the work was painted more than 20 years after van den Bosch's death in 1844, it is questionable whether the portrait is a true one. The painting is one of the Museum's earliest acquisitions, one of Raden Saleh's many donations.

PERAHU (BOAT)

Artist: Abas Alibasyah, born in
Purwakarta, West Java, 1928
Material: Oil on canvas
Size: 67 x 107 cm
Period: 1967
Inv. No: 02
Acquired: Date unknown

Abas Alibasyah has worked in this naturalistic style since 1942 when he joined the artists' organisation in Bandung during the Japanese Occupation. He is known not only as a painter, but also for his efforts in the struggle for Indonesia's independence. He received the Indonesian Medal of Honor (Satyalencana) in 1990.

MBAH IROSENTONO (OLD MAN IROSENTONO)

Artist: Trubus Sudarsono, born in
Wates, Central Java, 1926
Material: Oil on canvas
Size: 68.5 x 89 cm
Period: 1960
Inv. No: 232
Acquired: 1963

Trubus's paintings generally have a singular expressive substance—they present the human environment of Indonesia's traditional cultures. He is a self-taught painter who went on to teach at the Arts Academy of Indonesia in Yogyakarta from 1950 to 1965.

KAWAH DIENG (*DIENG PLATEAU*)
[LEFT TOP]

Artist: Widayat, born in Kutoharjo,
                  Central Java
Material: Oil on canvas
Size: 79 x 115 cm
Period: 1963
Inv. No: 258
Acquired: 1965

Widayat is one of Indonesia's
senior painters. He studied at the
Arts Institute of Indonesia in
Yogyakarta and subsequently
taught there. This painting shows
the naturalistic style Widayat
employed during the 1960s—very
different from the formal
visualization of his present
'decorative-magical' style.

KAWAH TANGKUBAN PERAHU (*MT. TANGKUBAN PERAHU CRATER*)
[LEFT BELOW]

Artist: Affandi, born in Cirebon, West
                  Java, 1907; d. 1990
Material: Oil on canvas
Size: 99 x 129 cm
Period: 1974
Inv. No: 05
Acquired: 1975

Affandi's work is known for his
vigorous application of paint—
sometimes with his hands or
straight from the tube, as in this
painting. He travelled widely in
Asia and Europe and was a leading
figure of the Indonesian
expressionist movement.

MERAPI YANG TAK KUNJUNG PADAM (*ETERNAL MERAPI*) [ABOVE]

Artist: Raden Basuki Abdullah, born
                  in Solo, Central Java, 1915; d.
                  1997
Material: Oil on canvas
Size: 150 x 200 cm
Period: 1992
Inv. No: 601
Acquired: 1993

R. Basuki Abdullah studied art in
Holland, Paris, and Rome. He was
known as a painter of the romantic
Mooi Indië school and remained
faithful to his choice of technique
and realist-naturalist style. He
became a skilled portraitist,
choosing as his subjects beautiful
women and heads of state.

FRAGMEN ABIMANYU (SCENE FROM ABIMANYU)

Artist:	Ida Bagus Made, born in Tebesaya, Ubud, Bali, 1915
Material:	Tempura on hardboard
Size:	65 x 120 cm
Period:	Unknown
Inv. No:	72
Acquired:	Date unknown

Ida Bagus Made is considered one of the main proponents of the Ubud style of painting. He also makes masks and sculpture for ritual use, rarely sells his work, and is known for his tough, eccentric character. This painting shows a scene from the 'Abimanyu' episode of the *Mahabharata*, reinterpreted in a Balinese setting, in an elaboration on the Kamasan style of classical Balinese painting.

GERHANA/DEWI RATIH (ECLIPSE/DEWI RATIH)

Artist:	I Gusti Ktut Kobot, born in Pengosekan, Ubud, Bali, 1917
Material:	Tempura on cloth
Size:	49 x 39 cm
Period:	1965
Inv. No:	39
Acquired:	1965

I Gusti Ktut Kobot, like Ida Bagus Made, was associated with the Pita Maha group in the 1930s. He is considered one of the pivotal artists working in the Ubud style. The painting recounts its narrative in a realistic manner while still managing to work in decorative motifs.

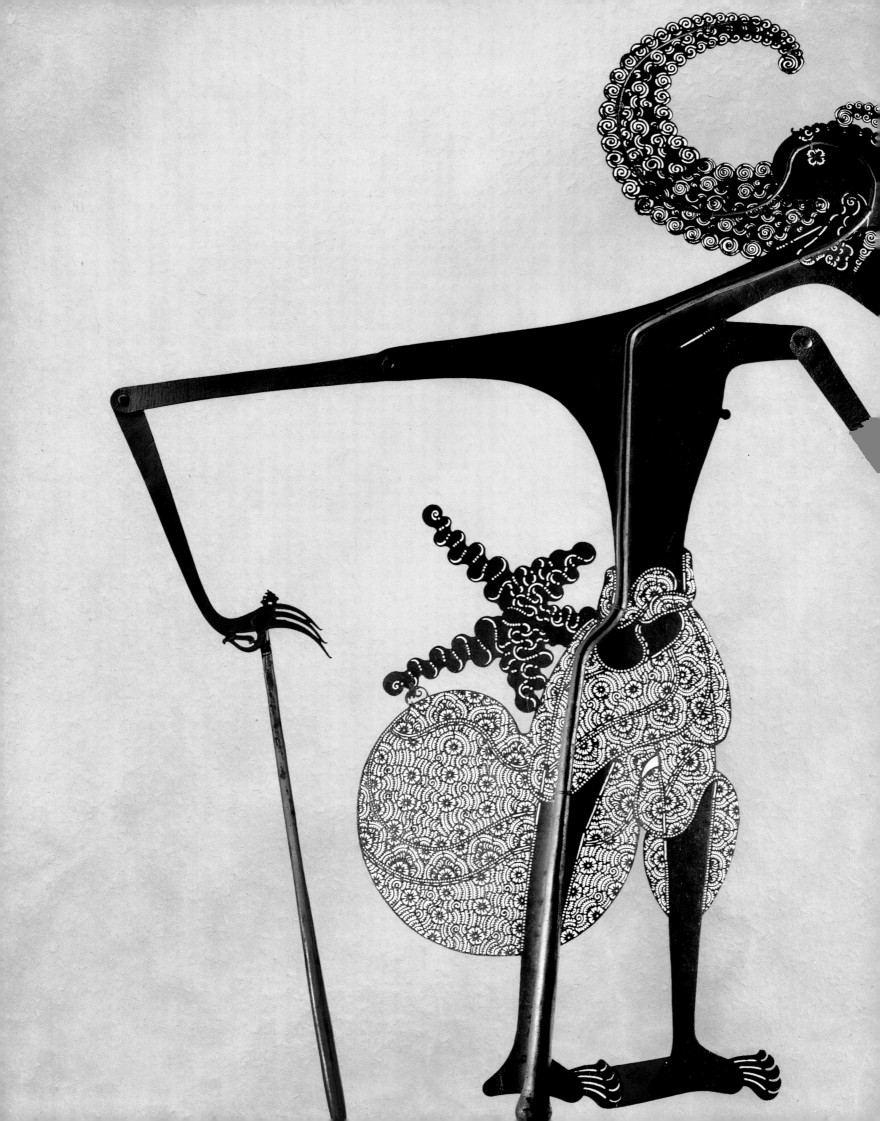

CHAPTER 8

PUPPETS AND MASKS

P uppets and masks are media through which ritual becomes theatre. There are two main streams of ritual theatre in Indonesia—the great *wayang* tradition that originated in the ancient kingdoms of Central Java; and the time-honoured rites of an underlying agrarian culture still found in the eastern islands of the archipelago. In some places the two streams co-exist; inevitably they intermingle.

Wayang is a very broad term encompassing not only puppets but also numerous theatrical forms, as well as referring to their actual performance. The meaning of the word *wayang* is in itself elusive— 'image', 'shadow'. The principal genres of *wayang* are shadow puppet theatre (*wayang kulit*), three-dimensional puppet theatre (*wayang golek*, with clothed puppets of wood), and dance-drama (*wayang wong*—'*wong*' meaning 'human being') that is sometimes performed with masks (*wayang topeng*).

Among these there are many variations with regard to theatrical convention, language, and literary sources, but there are several important aspects that all *wayang* forms share. All are accompanied by some form of gamelan music; all are based on a venerable literary text which is declaimed by certain types of characters; and all share a basic structure in which aristocratic heroes are opposed by high-ranking villains. Both 'sides' speak in an archaic poetic metre which is interpreted for the audience by clown-servants in the vernacular language. Most importantly, all *wayang* is to some degree a medium for moral and spiritual instruction. Its enduring popularity, throughout its many permutations, is due to the fact that it is also entertaining—and it appeals to a wide range of ages and levels of sophistication in a remarkable way. Rather than aiming for a broad middle ground, like much popular culture today, *wayang* appeals to different groups in different ways. Elderly literati enjoy the refinement of the poetry; intellectuals enjoy the social and philosophical issues; children enjoy the battle scenes; and everyone enjoys the clowns. Even foreigners who are unable to understand any of the languages can rejoice in the visual beauty of the plays.

The *Dalang*

Central to *wayang* is the puppeteer, the *dalang*, who manipulates the puppets, speaks for them in myriad voices, conducts the gamelan orchestra, and improvises the great stretches of the story where the clowns discuss the action of the play, as well as contemporary issues, in the vernacular language. A *dalang* is considered a spiritually powerful person. To perform *wayang* puppet theatre at all, requires great dexterity and musicianship, skill in the difficult art of chanting the ancient texts, and a prodigious memory. Moreover, he must be a good actor and storyteller—and if he is to have any success, he must be as funny as he is wise. Some forms of *wayang* have a direct ritual function, and in this case the *dalang* is also a priest with the power to create certain kinds of holy water. (In *wayang wong*, the narrator is referred to as a *dalang*, and requires the same skills of recitation.)

Ancient stories

The fundamental *wayang* form is *wayang kulit* (*kulit* meaning 'leather', from which the puppets are made). The leather is pierced to allow complex ornamentation, which helps to identify the several hundred different—sometimes only slightly different—puppets. The puppets are manipulated between a screen and a hanging lamp. The audience sitting in front of the screen sees only their shadows; but those who sit behind with the *dalang* and the orchestra see the puppets in all the beauty of their colours and gilding.

The literature of *wayang* is based mainly on the great Indian Hindu epics, the *Ramayana* and the *Mahabharata*—an immense literary, religious, and philosophical resource that for centuries has nourished poetry and the plastic arts as well. The Indonesian forms of these epics first appeared around a thousand years ago. *Wayang parwa*—which takes the form of puppet, masked, and danced theatre—is based on the *Mahabharata*. Javanese *wayang* also draws on a third stream of literature, known as the 'Panji' cycle, which originated in Indonesia. Another story cycle that appears in *wayang* is 'Damar Wulan', set in the time of Majapahit.

Regional variations abound in the vast tapestry of *wayang*. In Cirebon, West Java, a form of *wayang golek* developed, called *wayang golek cepak*, to give expression to the rising importance of Islam. ('*Cepak*' means 'flat', in reference to the flat-topped headdresses, like the *pici* caps worn by Muslim men.) Its vernacular language is Sundanese, rather than Javanese, and it recounts stories from the Islamic tradition. *Wayang klitik* puppets (also called *wayang krucil*), are carved from a flat piece of wood. The repertory is based on the Majapahit chronicles, told in the 'Damar Wulan' stories.

The performance of *wayang* in any of its forms is usually on the occasion of some ceremonial event—a wedding or circumcision or other rite of passage; in Bali it is often part of a temple festival. For all the ritual aspects of *wayang*, the context of the performance itself is informal and relaxed. The audience comes and goes, sometimes chatting, sometimes sleeping; food vendors do a lively business at the edge of the performance space. The plays usually take place at night and sometimes last until dawn.

The ritual use of masks cannot be entirely separated from the theatrical components of story and music. In Europe, the ritual source of modern theatre was articulated in the 1930s by the French dramatist Antonin Artaud when he developed his notion of a 'theatre of cruelty'. It was inspired by the *barong*-mask trance drama of Bali.

SHADOW PUPPET (*WAYANG KULIT*)
From Cirebon, West Java, this puppet is principally
made of leather (with paint and gilt applied),
wood, and horn.
Size: 76 cm high; *Inv. No*: 23510/82; *Acquired*: 1939

*This character is Arjuna, one of the five
principal heroes of the* Mahabharata.

The two figures above are from the Ramayana *epic. The villain appears on the* dalang's *left.*

WAYANG KULIT/KUMBAKARNA
Origin: Cirebon, Central Java
Material: Leather (paint and gilt),
           wood, horn
Size: 48 cm high
Inv. No: 23510 (17)
Acquired: 1939

WAYANG KULIT/PRABU DASAMUKA
Origin: Cirebon, Central Java
Material: Leather (paint and gilt),
           wood, horn
Size: 50 cm high
Inv. No: 23510 (19)
Acquired: 1939

Shown (from left to right) are figures from the Mahabharata—*Arjuna, Werkudara, and Yudhistira.*

WAYANG KULIT
Origin: Cirebon, West Java
Material: Leather (paint and gilt),
           wood, horn
Acquired: 1939

ARJUNA
Size: 76 cm high
Inv. No: 23510/82

WERKUDARA
Size: 92 cm high
Inv. No: 23510/21

YUDHISTIRA
Size: 78 cm high
Inv. No: 23510/91

WAYANG GOLEK CEPAK
Origin: Cirebon, West Java
Material: Painted wood, bamboo,
            cotton cloth
Size: 46 cm
Inv. No: 22114
Acquired: 1937

This puppet is Patih Mangku Yuda.

WAYANG GOLEK [LEFT]

Origin: Sukabumi, West Java
Material: Painted wood, bamboo,
           cotton cloth
Size: 47 cm high
Inv. No: 21233 (2)
Acquired: 1936

This is Darmakusuma, a king of the
Indraprasta kingdom and a
reincarnation of Hyang Darma
who, it is said, lived until the rise
of the Islamic kingdom of Demak
in the 16th century.

WAYANG KLITIK [BELOW]

Origin: Java
Material: Painted wood, bamboo,
           buffalo leather
Size: 50 cm high; 21 cm wide
Inv. No: 27242
Acquired: 1954

The flat wooden *wayang klitik*
puppet here is the character
Menak Curing.

These four masks depict characters from the 'Panji' stories. They are called topeng daleman, *or courtiers' masks, because they are used in dances performed only by members of the nobility and court servants ('dalem' refers to the inner sanctum of the palace).*

TOPENG WAYANG WONG
Origin: Yogyakarta, Central Java
Material: Painted wood, semi-precious
               stones, animal skin
Acquired: 1938

PANJI ASMORO BANGUN [TOP LEFT]
Size: 17.5 x 14 cm
Inv. No: 22255 (38)

RAGIL KUNING [TOP RIGHT]
Size: 17.5 x 13.5 cm
Inv. No: 22255 (34)

DEWOKUSUMO [BOTTOM RIGHT]
Size: 18 x 14 cm
Inv. No: 22255 (41)

JAYENG ANDOGO [OPPOSITE]
Size: 18 x 13.5 cm
Inv. No: 22255 (20)

TOPENG CIREBON [RIGHT]

Origin: Cirebon, West Java
Material: Painted wood
Size: 18 x 16 cm
Inv. No: 20189
Acquired: 1932

A 'grotesque' mask portraying the character Buta Terong. A *buta* is a creature representing the lower orders of human character, such as greed or dim-wittedness.

TOPENG MALANG [BELOW]

Origin: Malang, East Java
Material: Painted wood
Size: 22 x 18 cm
Inv. No: 23191
Acquired: 1938

This character, Bapang, is known by his coarse manner and uproarious laughter.

***BARONG LANDUNG/*'JERO LUH'**

Origin: Bali
Material: Painted wood
Size: 19.8 x 14.2 cm
Inv. No: 25945
Acquired: 1942

Barong landung are a pair of large male-female guardian figures, very sacred to the Balinese and viewed only on special ritual occasions. The male, 'Jero Gede', has a black face; the female's 'Jero Luh', is white. The full-figure effigies are nearly three metres high when they are paraded (*landung* means 'tall'). These giant puppets are animated by priests; they dance slightly and sing to each other from old bawdy poetry. The origins of this form are obscure, but there are associations with a legendary Chinese princess who was married to the demonic king Mayadanawa. Other myths connect the pair to the fanged demon 'Batara Macaling', the purveyor of cholera, said to live on the nearby island of Nusa Penida.

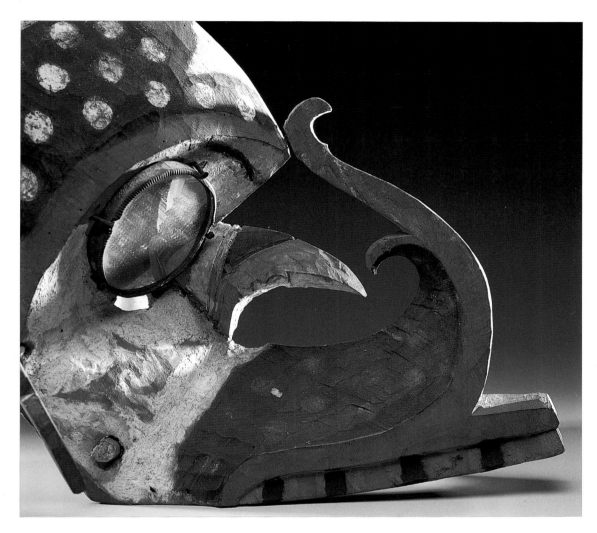

TOPENG BATAK KARO [OPPOSITE]

Origin: Raja village, Simalungan, North Sumatra
Material: Painted wood, palm fibre, animal hide
Size: 61 x 25 cm
Inv. No: 14195
Acquired: 1910

This highly expressive mask would have been worn for burial rites for only the most high-ranking personage, such as a king. In former times, burials would be accompanied by music and the sacrifice, sometimes dramatised, of a slave, to attend the king in his journey into the afterlife.

TOPENG HUDOQ [ABOVE AND RIGHT]

Origin: Dayak Kenyah, Apo Kayan, East Kalimantan
Material: Soft wood, mirrors, animal hide
Size: 38 x 25 cm
Inv. No: 12057
Acquired: 1905

This mask, or *budot*, is worn in the *hudoq* ritual dance, performed as part of rites associated with the rice-growing cycle. *Hudoq* is performed by male dancers and a leader (*pawang*). The imagery of the mask is a composite of dangerous animals and crop pests, meant to frighten by imitation.

APPENDICES

The nearly 110,000 items of the National Museum's collection are presently under the care of two main curatorial branches—Prehistory & Anthropology, and History & Archaeology—which in turn are divided into four sub-sections each. These curatorial departments have been developed over time and their activities have become more precisely defined. As research and museum theory evolve, the classification of objects is subject to occasional revision. However, the principal classifications of the collection, as they currently stand, are listed on the following page.

The objects gathered beneath the roof of the National Museum are so impressive that they speak for themselves—but the curators of the National Museum play a vital part in the preservation, research and display of the Nation's priceless collection. On the following pages the curators share their thoughts about the collection, their work, their efforts towards increasing public education about the collections, as well as their hopes for the National Museum's future development.

THE COLLECTIONS AND THE CURATORS

PREHISTORY (41,896 items)
Objects from Indonesia's Paleolithic, Neolithic, and Bronze ages until the emergence of writing in the archipelago around the 5th century AD. The items include stone implements (axes, adzes); earthenware; objects made of bone, shell, and horn; bronze tools, ornaments, and ceremonial objects. This is by far the largest of the museum's collections; it is further divided into 17 categories.

ARCHAEOLOGY (14,196 items)
Objects from the Hindu-Buddhist cultures of the classical Indonesian period, from the emergence of writing to the rise of Islam (7th-15th century). The collection consists of stone and bronze religious statuary and ceremonial objects; stone inscriptions (*prasasti*); musical instruments; coins; ornaments and jewellery; and domestic objects. Much of the collection, including the celebrated Wonoboyo hoard, was found in Central or East Java.

HISTORICAL RELICS (410 items)
Objects from the 16th-19th century, a period which saw a great influx of Europeans, mostly Dutch, Portuguese, and English. The items consist of household furnishings, weapons, bells, and other objects associated with Indonesia's history during this period.

NUMISMATICS AND HERALDRY (17,112 items)
Coins and paper money from Indonesia, Europe, Africa, America, Australia, and Asia, from prehistory to the present. The heraldic collection comprises coats of arms, seals, medals, and other official documents, from the Dutch colonial period to the present.

Included in this division, but sometimes standing independently is the collection of inscriptions and manuscripts (*naskah*)—written documents in a number of languages and scripts, in such materials as paper, parchment, bark, barkcloth, lontar and nipa palm leaf, rattan, and bamboo.

GEOGRAPHY (583 items)
This collection comprises fossils, stones and botanical and zoological specimens of the Indonesian archipelago, as well as geographical equipment, and a collection of maps dating from the 16th-19th century.

ETHNOGRAPHY (29,500 items)
A large and various collection, reflecting the archipelago's great ethnic diversity. Sub-collections include textiles; musical instruments; puppets and masks; domestic implements such as looms and farming and fishing tools; and ritual objects, weapons, and personal ornaments that are specific to an ethnic group's identity.

CERAMICS (5,513 items)
The very great majority of this collection is the foreign ceramics collection (5,056) founded by E.W. van Orsoy de Flines and donated to the museum in 1959: the pieces, which date from the Han Dynasty (200 BC) to the Qing Dynasty (19th century), were all found in Indonesia, and they provide important clues about the history of Indonesia's trade relations.

FINE ARTS (450 items)
This collection consists of two- and three-dimensional works of art by Indonesian and foreign artists of the modern period, beginning in the mid-19th century with Raden Saleh and continuing to the present. Some of the foreign works in this

collection were gifts of state, such as the lithographs on these pages, which were presented to the Nation by the French Government in 1959.

The curators of the National Museum are responsible for researching and describing the items of the collection in their particular fields, and presenting the objects to the public through exhibitions and publications. They work in coordination with the museum's departments of Conservation and Preparation and of Education and Publishing.

Here the curators discuss the pleasures and challenges of their work.

Dra. SUWATI KARTIWA, MSc.
Director of the National Museum
Special expertise: Textiles

'Besides their high aesthetic value, Indonesian textiles reveal much about Indonesian culture. I am especially interested in the philosophical meanings to be found in the motifs and designs. This is the greatest pleasure for me—seeing the beauty of the textiles and the sophistication of the weavers' work. The greatest challenge is that not all the collections have been examined and analyzed, and there is much research still to do.'

Dra. SUHARDINI CHALID
Prehistory & Anthropology Department

'Studying the collections is very rewarding because as one learns about the background of the objects, one discovers a great deal about how different people live—their beliefs, history, and customs—and gains a larger picture of human life and culture. The difficulty is that part of the collection was acquired 100 to 150 years ago, with very little documentation. It is a big challenge for the curator to gather information about these objects and about the context in which they were made and used.'

Dra. HARI BUDIARTI
Ethnography

'Working at the museum demands a commitment, which I find

personally fulfilling. I enjoy studying the cultural products of the various Indonesian ethnic groups. They are often surprising and beautiful. The collection is enormous, and so the responsibility is also very great. The work is demanding in that it requires one to be thorough and precise; and one must be patient in the task of obtaining complete data.'

Dra. WAHYU ERNAWATI
Ethnography

'As a curator, one gets to know a wider world—partly through the collections, which are a way of learning about some of Indonesia's extraordinary ethnic groups—and partly through the museum's activities. I especially enjoy visiting other museums, both in Indonesia and abroad. The greatest challenges are maintaining harmony within the demands of a diverse working environment; and finding the means to carry out field research and conduct comparative studies in other museums.'

Drs. R. DWI NUGROHO G.
Ethnography

'Having a background in anthropology, I feel that I must be especially energetic in studying the collections and working as a team with my colleagues in the museum. I enjoy mounting exhibitions, attending seminars, working on publications and visiting the regional museums around the archipelago.'

Dra. RODINA SATRIANA
Ethnography

'My background is in anthropology and my special interest is in textiles and traditional dress. The collections allow one the privilege of imagination and discovery—visualising how the different peoples of Indonesia lived in earlier times is the most important part of my research. I believe that one of the important issues facing the Nation's collection in the 21st century is keeping the objects in properly controlled conditions and free of dust so that fragile items are not ruined. The enlargement of the museum should help tremendously this essential matter.'

Dra. INTAN MARDIANA NAPITUPULU
Archaeology

'The Archaeology collection holds information about how people lived long ago, and by studying it we can add to our knowledge of the past. I enjoy researching the background of the collection, communicating information to visitors, and planning exhibitions so that they will appeal to visitors of all levels of society. The challenge is to make the best possible possible use of the collections.'

Dra. DEDAH R. SRI HANDARI
Prehistory

'The Prehistory collection is very big. Of its 41,896 items, only 819 have ever been exhibited; and there are special challenges involved in researching, storing, and exhibiting so many objects, especially given the great diversity of their origins and of the objects themselves. At the same time, the greatest pleasure is when, in the course of researching an object, one is able to imagine or visualize the people who once made or used it. This leads one to search further to uncover the mystery.'

DIANI PURWANDARI, BA
Prehistory

'Because my background is in archaeology, I am especially interested in the Prehistory collection. One of my greatest pleasures is the task of researching the collection; but because of its great size and diversity, this is also my biggest challenge. I believe that we must organize our research to allow us to travel to make comparative studies with other collections all over the world.'

Dra. EKOWATI SUNDARI
Ceramics

'The Ceramics collection is valuable for its archaeological data as well as the artistic merit of the objects. What I enjoy most about my work in caring for this collection is the research—analysis, description, and writing; comparative studies; and communicating with other specialists. What I find most challenging is the great number of items in the collection that I have not yet been able to study.'

Drs. BUDI PRIHATNA
Ethnography

'As I see it, my fundamental responsibility as a curator is to give the public the widest possible information about the collection. This can take several different forms. It may be in talking directly to visitors, or in publications, or helping other organizations, such as the Indonesian Heritage Society.'

Drs. WAHYONO MARTOWIKRIDO
History & Archaeology Department

'My responsibilities are many and varied, from checking the collection, advising the director and overseeing the curators to writing

articles. The greatest pleasure for me is in working closely with beautiful objects. The greatest challenge is in communicating to society the meaning of a particular object.'

Drs. JUNAIDI ISMAIL
Geography (old maps)

'With maps one is able to get to know different places around the world without having to travel. What I enjoy best is researching the collection and writing descriptions of items. I'm sure that I would also enjoy fieldwork. The most challenging part of my job is reading the old Dutch texts associated with the maps. Also, there seems to be a lack of material published in Indonesian about these regions and about world geography in general.'

Drs. TRIGANGGA
Numismatics

'The study of coins has broadened my perception of the history of other countries. Among the 17,112 pieces in the Numismatics collection, I am particularly interested in old Javanese coins and those that are irregular or rare. My greatest pleasure in this job is the feeling of satisfaction when I am able to complete my work on schedule.'

Dra. PENI MUDJI SUKATI
Historical Relics

'I find great satisfaction in dealing with the Historical Relics collection and researching the background of the objects. It feel that I am on a path that leads to a greater understanding of not only the past but also the present. Among my duties, what I enjoy most is finding new information or data about the collection. What I find most challenging is researching texts in Dutch.'

Drs. TUBAGUS ANDRE SUKMANA
Fine Arts

'I have been drawn to the arts ever since I was a schoolboy, and my background training is in fine arts. My responsibilities include, among other things, examining the visual structure and expressive substance of the collection and compiling biographical data about the artists. This requires not only a broad knowledge of art but an aesthetic faculty as well, and I enjoy being able to apply my abilities in my work. The challenge is to increase one's skills, especially in the knowledge of art history, museum management, and foreign languages—and to make the public more aware of the importance of the museum.'

Drs. SUBIYANTO
Education and Publishing

'My job is generally to convey information about the collections to schools, universities, the general public, and official guests. This includes activities within the museum and a "museum on wheels" that travels to elementary schools around West Java. My greatest pleasure is when visitors express satisfaction with what our department has done for them. The biggest challenge is looking after guests who do not speak English.

Other curators who contributed to this book but were unable to participate in the interview are: Drs. Teguh Hari Susanto, Haryianti, Drs. Sutrisno, and Dra. Istigomah; from the secretarial staff: Drs. Asrul Basri; Drs. Budi Priadi, Ety Sulastri, BA, Paulina Suitella, BA

Opposite page: This untitled lithograph (59.5 x 47.5 cm) by the Russian-born artist Wassily Kandinsky (1866-1944) was made in 1935 and was a gift of the French Government to the Government of Indonesia (1959). Inv. No: C.84-364-56f.

Above left: An untitled lithograph (59.5 x 47.5 cm) by the modern Hungarian artist Victor Vasarely. Gift of the French Government (1959). Inv. No: .78-386-104b.

Above right: A lithograph (65.5 x 50 cm) by Sonia Delaunay (1885-1979) from 1958. Gift of the French Government (1959). Inv. No: . 27-470-34a.

Left: An untitled lithograph (60 x 47.5 cm) by the German artist Hans Hartung. Inv. No: .31-484-50a.

INDEX

Page numbers in italics indicate illustrations

ACKNOWLEDGEMENTS
The photographs in this book were taken by
Tara Sosrowardoyo, with the following
exceptions:

photographs by Beck Tohir, pages 6, 8, 9;
from the collection of the National Museum,
pages 10, 11, 12-13, 18, 22, 23, 24 , 26, 27,
28; by courtesy of John Falconer, pages 14,
15, 16, 17, 20, 21, 25, 29; from the
collection of Editions Didier Millet, page 19.